MW01146790

NO SENSE IN WISHING

NO SENSE IN WISHING

Essays

LAWRENCE BURNEY

ATRIA BOOKS

New York   Amsterdam/Antwerp   London
Toronto   Sydney/Melbourne   New Delhi

ATRIA
BOOKS

An Imprint of Simon & Schuster, LLC
1230 Avenue of the Americas
New York, NY 10020

First Atria Books hardcover edition July 2025

ATRIA BOOKS and colophon are trademarks of Simon & Schuster, LLC

Simon & Schuster strongly believes in freedom of expression and stands against censorship in all its forms. For more information, visit BooksBelong.com.

For information about special discounts for bulk purchases, please contact Simon & Schuster Special Sales at 1-866-506-1949 or business@simonandschuster.com.

The Simon & Schuster Speakers Bureau can bring authors to your live event. For more information or to book an event, contact the Simon & Schuster Speakers Bureau at 1-866-248-3049 or visit our website at www.simonspeakers.com.

Interior design by Yvonne Taylor

Manufactured in the United States of America

1 3 5 7 9 10 8 6 4 2

Library of Congress Cataloging-in-Publication Data

ISBN 978-1-6680-5185-6
ISBN 978-1-6680-5187-0 (ebook)

For my late grandmother,
Sandra Lee.

CONTENTS

INTRODUCTION XI

A VERY PRECIOUS TIME 1

GLORY 19

MY KING, MY FATHER 35

A LOVE LETTER TO STEAMED CRABS
PILED ONTO A BED OF NEWSPAPER 49

TWO PILLARS 61

REVISITING RAMONA 83

FAKE DIFFERENT 103

GOOD GOVERNMENT JOB 119

MR. MOONEY & THE COMPLEXION
FOR THE PROTECTION 129

BRUISED 143

THE EXCHANGE 165

CONTENTS

WELCOME HOME   175

TIME IS VERY PRECIOUS   199

MIKE's WORLD   213

SALUTATIONS   225

NO SENSE
IN WISHING

INTRODUCTION

THIS ISN'T THE BOOK I thought I'd write if ever afforded the opportunity. For more than a decade now, my work has been mostly concerned with trying to tell other people's stories, in the hopes of painting a compelling and thoughtful portrait of Black life and how it's reflected through creative expression. I've tracked the evolution of music coming out of my home region at a time when the sonics were shifting from homegrown subgenres to locally informed hip-hop once the influence of social media became unavoidable. I've hopped in the car and taken road trips all around the United States to catch artists right at the sweet spot of transitioning from hometown heroes to performers with national promise. And when the chance came, I boarded flights to the Motherland to see what distant relatives were trying to push out to the rest of the world, artistically. The role of a culture journalist, from what I was taught, wasn't necessarily to perform objectivity; we all have our slants. But, at the very least, it was to not get in the way of readers feeling like they were in the same room as an artist, thinker, or movement they've been craving a deeper access to and understanding of. So, that's what I set out to do. The book I thought I'd write was going to be somewhere along those lines: me in another person's world depicting them in their natural state, only showing myself enough to let it be known they're having a conversation with a fellow human being. A different way showed itself to me, though.

In this life, we endure an infinite series of experiences that change us at the molecular level. The first song that had a lasting impression on you isn't likely the first memory you have of a song, but something about the one you *do* remember changes you in considerable ways. Just like the first time you sat with a book that made you say to yourself, "I have to change the course of my life after reading this." This book is an exercise in mining the memory for those path-altering episodes. It is not necessarily concerned with retelling events for history's sake, though there will be instances of that in these pages. Memory is something different. It is how our brains and hearts—when exposed to the elements of our environment—process history. The way I remember having a crab feast at my grandmother's house may get the number of crabs, the people present, or the tablecloth we ate on wrong. What isn't wrong is the effect the experience had on me and why, when I eat crabs to this day, I associate the act with intimacy and fellowship.

In these pages you'll find me contending with instances in my life when a song, a film, an artist, something in my neighborhood, or a side conversation I overheard led me to transformative revelations. What you read may or may not reflect specific experiences you've had. Not everybody can lay claim to a life-altering car accident or how a film that popped up on their algorithm made them reflect on their shortcomings as a father. But I can assure you, what you will connect to is how the things we absorb change us. All the changes laid out here won't be flowery and neatly concluded with happy endings. Though they do take place, happy endings are not common in the human experience. I want to be reflective of that universal truth. Because what we digest can also bring us a fair share of agony and confusion.

At the present, there's a crisis of misinformation swirling around our digital communities—misinformation that turns people's desire to learn and find meaning against them. I am hoping that taking the leap to share my truths and experiences while lining them up against the myths we are sold about ourselves, neighbors, and supposed enemies will help to weaken their foundations. I hope, in chronicling how I perceive the world, I do not come off as self-centered or self-serving, but rather as someone with a deep desire to connect. That way, I can feel a bit more rational in my thoughts. And what better way to pursue that than to draw links between my life and others to what is happening in the cultural sphere? No other form of production in our society best reflects the current state of the human condition: its wants, its need for domination, its methods of manipulation, and its fight to rid itself of guilt, or pain. I offer *No Sense in Wishing* as a plea with myself to finally look at what's around me, interact with it, and send out dispatches from the conversations that are produced. And I hope it will bring conversation back to me.

A VERY PRECIOUS TIME

S ELECTIVE MEMORY IS A funny thing, especially when you're a casualty of it. Gil Scott-Heron resented the idea that, by the late nineties, he'd withered away into some drugged-out has-been whose best years were behind him. The man who'd worked tirelessly through all the seventies and half the eighties screaming out to the world with that trembling timbre, wiry frame, and full-bodied 'fro in hopes that, maybe, some of our wounds could be mended, was being conveniently relegated to the past tense. "I didn't know it until I read it in the reviews that I was dead or something," he told the *Houston Press* in September of '98 while on a resurgent press run. "That's where they put you when they don't see you."

If the barometer for living was how often one releases new music, Gil had been dead to many for well over a decade. *Spirits*, from 1994, was breezed over. Before that, he hadn't put out an official album in America since '82. Out of the spotlight, he gigged when he felt like, taught at colleges, recorded live albums that were released in Europe, and wrote. But there was renewed momentum behind him in '98. Months before speaking with the *Houston Press*, Gil reissued 1974's *Winter in America* on CD

1

through his own label, Rumal-Gia Records. The record was the first of many he made in collaboration with pianist and flautist Brian Jackson. Its being distributed on CD—followed by reissues of *From South Africa to South Carolina* and *The First Minute of a New Day* later that year—meant Gil had a chance to become more accessible to a new audience that needed to hear the ways he reasoned with the world through his jazzy, poetically spirited brand of soul music.

Winter in America was a developmental jump for Scott-Heron as an artist. His work up to that point positioned him as a refreshingly analytical poet whose resonant and dynamic portraits of Black American life were sometimes accompanied by backing music. But Brian Jackson's involvement on this album gave those messages a tonal foundation from which his songs could be absorbed in a new—and more profound—way. Scott-Heron lent his voice to exploring his community's fullness over a beautifully crisp sonic quality, but Jackson's contributions to a multilayered sound amplified those sentiments in ways words could not. Tender piano solos at the start of songs reel you in, so that when Scott-Heron's cries about needing a sign to lead him out of a wayward funk, you're hit right in the chest upon arrival. The busyness of frantic keystrokes and drum taps adds urgency to stories about needing to get out of the city to go visit family in the sticks, where life's a bit more forgiving. Like hip-hop would do decades after, the album added irresistible decoration to feelings of Black existential anguish, but also Black existential hope and gratitude.

The album was made for people whose stories ended prematurely on unforgiving city streets. Or at the very least, the album was, in a roundabout way, inspired by the spirit they carried. And not just in a metaphorical sense. Gil shuffled through similar blocks as he constructed these stories. In the early stages of putting the album together, he was a graduate student at Johns Hopkins writing seminars in Baltimore, just a short stroll from the bustle of the city's Eastside hoods. When Brian Jackson came down from New York to start the album, he met the artist Eugene Cole, a teacher at Morgan State University, through mutual friends at a party. Jackson introduced Cole to Gil, and Gil commissioned Cole to make *Winter in America*'s cover art. The psychedelic landscape Cole made was built around a photo he'd taken in Baltimore of a man wearing the same exact suit he had pawned not long before—a solitary somber-eyed figure staring off into the distance. The album was recorded in Silver Spring, Maryland, about forty-five minutes south of Baltimore. Its lead single was inspired by drunks hanging out in front of Gil's neighborhood liquor store when he stayed in DC right after leaving Hopkins. Maybe it's my urge to engage in ethnocentrism that gives Gil's stint in my home region an added dimension of sentimentality, but really it's incredibly sound reporting. Those mid-Atlantic avenues acted as muses for his dispatches of Black life as people were experiencing the consequences of broken promises; promises assuring a more dignified existence waiting at home for veterans upon their return from combat; promises of better days from elders, government officials, and preachers that just never came. He could likely have pulled that same story together from any other corner of the country. Nevertheless, those repeated blows to the prospects of security and optimism for

Black Americans are very much in the tremble of Scott-Heron's voice throughout *Winter in America.*

That single he crafted bearing witness to his DC neighbors' collective unraveling is "The Bottle." Following three central figures in a place that could be wherever you're from or anywhere else where negroes reside in the rural South, urban North, or postindustrial Midwest, Gil dissects what often meets his eye. First, he observed the steady demise of a man in his neighborhood who had fallen so deep into alcoholism that he became a terror to the people who loved him most. His son hated to see him coming, shuffling down the street slurring words in a barely decipherable jibber-jabber. The man pawned everything of value he could get ahold of, including his wife's wedding ring. As the groove builds around Jackson's fluting, attentive hips loosen to the tambourine while Gil continues to survey the area. Next in view: a woman whose radiance gradually dulled after her man was sent to prison. In a moment of alcohol-induced judgment, she cracks a preacher upside the head with the liquorless vessel from which her fix came. Later in the track: a doctor that used to perform abortions on teen girls who couldn't get health care anywhere else starts to wander the streets in a drunken stupor after his operation was deemed unlawful and shut down. There's no real resolve here, which actually gives the song's message a bit more of a kick. As much of his work achieved before, and would after, it's an indictment of a society leaving many of its citizens to rot when they're no longer of use.

For *Winter in America*'s initial release in '74, "The Bottle" kicks off the B-side of the record. It's a noticeably more hysterical track, energetically, than anything else on the album; "A Very Precious Time" opens with a ninety-second keyboard solo from Brian Jackson before Gil bellows out, reflecting on the euphoria of early-stage romance; "Rivers of My Fathers," though more doleful, starts similarly. There, he yearns for a retreat from the unkind circumstances he's found himself in. So much of *Winter in America* falls along those lines—Scott-Heron acting as a vessel of acutely felt discontentment. But on "The Bottle," instead of singing in a downtrodden voice, he rides the beat more like a rap. This approach emphasizes the desperation he sees around him.

As a writer, Gil's greatest gift was finding language that got to the heart of what drives people to the edge of sanity, where many slip into the bottomless pit. There's credible concern in the way he says, "His old man got a problem," before adding, "and it's a bad one." But there's still a sense of powerlessness as to add emphasis to how much of a crisis it really is. "The Bottle" contends with our society's propensity to wave off addicts as people whose depth goes no further than what immediately meets the eye, rather than acknowledging a brutal truth: that life has a tendency to throw shit at us that we're not often equipped to handle without self-medicating.

While Gil breaks it down to a science, Brian Jackson commands such a sacred control of the flute that he offers soothing, albeit short-lived, distraction from the tragedies. The beat so sprightly it makes it so your body won't be able to resist rhythmically stepping through a horrifying story of human deterioration. The melodies grow more and more urgent as Gil depicts how this father, woman, and doctor become shells of their former selves. Some of Gil's anguish feels like it comes from knowing how close he, and most people in the communities that he's lived in, are to being sung about in this way—even if just *one* thing takes a sharp, unexpected turn for the worst.

"The Bottle" is also the song my mother, Victoria, most associated with the lanky Chicago-born poet during her childhood in West Baltimore. Hanging in the attic of her grandparents' house on Park Heights and Wiley, her uncle Macky would break down herb on vinyl album covers and listen to Gil's music while practicing on his drum set. To her, Gil was a scraggly rebel in comparison to the angelic presentations of Stevie Wonder, Marvin Gaye, or Al Green. "Sound like he need to put a damn sweater on," my aunt Chee Chee, who preferred pristine-sounding brothers, would half-jokingly remark about Gil's not-so-singerly delivery to my teen mother. But regardless of his ragamuffin appearance, "The Bottle" was too irresistible of a track for my mother to overlook, as it got more radio play than anything else he'd released up to that point.

When my mother graduated from high school in the early eighties and had my sister shortly after, she started working at an avant-garde clothing store called Scratch-n-Sniff in Mount Vernon, a centrally located part of White Baltimore where alternative negroes also hang. In her spare time, she sang backup in a reggae band called Jah Rising, which played a combination of covers and original songs. But at Scratch-n-Sniff, her coworkers played the Smiths, Depeche Mode, Joy Division, and U2. She started befriending British DJs who, for reasons I can't fathom, found themselves in this raggedy port city, and she also briefly ended up with a gangly, well-read white boyfriend named Bobby, whom she met in the shop. It was through building relationships with these bohemians that my mother came back in contact with Gil Scott-Heron's music, which she could now enjoy with her adult experiences as points of entry. She bought *Winter in America* from a record store and with new, artfully wired ears that could appreciate who he was beyond his lone commercial hit. Beyond her memory of a radical guy whose music was in constant rotation in Uncle Macky's attic bedroom, she connected to how Gil told our stories with supreme care, which was paramount for her as a young adult and a new mother.

Despite (or, perhaps, because of) being counterculture, Gil Scott-Heron actually had more intergenerational relevance than a good plenty of his peers with household names. Scattered all over the living rooms, attics, porches, stoops, and street corners of this country, little Black children like my mother were soaking in Gil's charismatic truth telling, their sonic education being introduced by cool uncles, cousins, neighbors, parents, and teachers. When those little Black children matured, Gil's influence seeped into the growing popularity of their new hip-hop culture in the late eighties and early nineties. Kids, mostly in their late teens and early twenties, began profusely sampling his seventies output— his proto-rap vocal style and tendency to speak plainly rather than metaphorically appealed to youth's evergreen inclination to be antiestablishment with ease.

Beyond the slick delivery, what I believe those young Gen X poets connected to most was Gil's relentless questioning of how America's sociopolitical structure would impact them, and his warnings of how they could be used as pawns in that system. They felt accounted for in his work, cradled by him simply saying, *Wait, this shit ain't right and I can't go another day without letting it be known, jack*—or however brothers would have phrased that in the days of perfectly round 'fros and sufficiently tailored jeans. So, to me, it makes sense that when the Jungle Brothers recruited Q-Tip on "Black Is Black" for a story about how, in the late eighties, the only thing different about being Black from OG's time is that people were mystified by the new-and-improved covert ways of oppression, they sampled "The Bottle." Or how KRS-One used elements of "The Revolution Will Not Be Televised" to produce Queen Latifah's "Evil That Men Do," where she explored the ways in which her male counterparts, regardless of race, had a habit of disregarding struggles particular to women. Or even how when a young Prodigy accepted that an early grave was the only logical consequence for his morally corrupt lifestyle on Mobb Deep's "If It's Alright," *Winter in America*'s title track laid the production's foundation. The inquisitive and intuitive spirit of Gil's social commentary was transferable, and adaptable enough to hold up against updated versions of the ills he saw in his own youth.

By 1998, in her mid-thirties, my mother had off-and-on stints with a few groups in Baltimore's underground Black music and poetry spaces. One of which was Wolfpack, a quartet composed of her as the lead vocalist, my grandfather (Pop) on guitar or drums, his buddy Mr. Skeets, who looked like the light-skin, human version of a Russian wolfhound, on the keys, and Mr. Greg, who had long dreads, dressed like Carlos Santana, and was the first person I ever knew with a white wife, on the bass. This was a cohort of people who may have, at one point, wanted to make it big. But at this stage of life, they just needed to jam on the regular for their own well-being. My grandfather was a life-long musician who, during my infancy in the early nineties, got to experience the out-of-body high of drumming for Parliament-Funkadelic on two European tours. But he was mostly paid in drugs and came back to Baltimore to drive cabs and help my grandmother with bills. In need of playing, he orchestrated a whole music universe in our basement on Aisquith Street, where artists would come rock out until my grandmother got sick of the noise, practicing for whatever shows on the local circuit they'd get called up for. Wolfpack kind of disbanded when Mr. Greg had another group he wanted to play with, so Pop moved over to guitar and a young dude named Lamont took over drums, the updated outfit mostly taking on small gigs around the city and sticking to after-work rehearsals. But their Baltimore scene status was legitimized by a December 1998 benefit show at a newly Black-run spot called the Heritage Shadows of the Silver Screen Museum & Cinema on North Avenue. Pop's buddy Art Woodard, who booked jazz shows in the Baltimore-DC region, called him up and asked, "What band you playing with now? I got something for you." The nameless band confirmed interest and was added to the lineup, placed as the opener for a headlining act that inspired them to get their shit straight with a heightened sense of urgency.

An Unplugged Benefit

For The Heritage Shadows of the Silver Screen Museum & Cinema

Featuring

"A Message to the Messengers"

GIL SCOTT-HERON

And Introducing Balto's Newest Vocal Sensation:

"VICTORIA"

Saturday, December 5, 1998

(Performances at 8 p.m. and 11 p.m.)

is what the printed grayscale flyer, featuring in the background a photo of Scott-Heron wearing a black beret and turtleneck with his arms folded, read. Pop, "Victoria," Mr. Skeets, and Lamont upped rehearsal hours in our East Baltimore basement in respect for the gravity of the occasion. The collectively decided setlist taped on the wall kept them sharp.

Heritage Shadows of the Silver Screen Museum & Cinema wasn't a proper music venue. It wasn't even a functioning museum or theater; just a mostly vacant Italian Renaissance Revival–style movie house from the early 1900s with aspirations of being a haven for Baltimore's majority-Black population. Proceeds from the show's $25 tickets were to go toward making it the nation's first museum and cinema devoted to African Americans in film. Saturday night's event was in the building's lobby in an intimate setup, the performers at eye level with their audience. With nowhere to drop eight-year-old me off, I was dragged along to the gig. The visual details of this night are fuzzy, but I would bet $50 that, while sitting among adults at a white-clothed round table, an older gentleman with oval-shaped shades looked at me and said, "Aight now, young fella," extending his arm and closed fist out for a pound. From a photograph my mother still owns, I know I wore a royal blue T-shirt under a pair of denim overalls. And my cheeks still had prepubescent fat on them, rounding out my face.

Pop, Mr. Skeets, and Lamont opened without my mother for about three tracks or so to get the blood flowing. When she joined them, her first selection was an upbeat number, probably covering something by Lalah Hathaway. But I do remember the one that grabbed the crowd by their back collars, because whenever I tagged along for shows, it conjured up similar feelings: a cover of Oleta Adams's "Get Here." My mother's alto voice, when she hit notes requiring the most projection, could crack the sky open. The kind of carrying on that inspired head-tilting *Mmm!*'s from people who hadn't been to a church since Reagan was in office.

After their set, the band returned to our table, hyped up on adrenaline while trying to appear poised. When I caught Gil Scott-Heron's profile as he and his band organized their setup, I asked, "Ma, who is he?" The clear shift in the crowd's energy, the silent and focused attention on his every move, made it apparent that he was important. He was getting back into form, and the performance was a bit of a slow burn. He ran through the gems of his two-decades-long career, often offering in his silky-smooth deep voice anecdotal introductions that aligned with the following tune's message. One that stuck out was a story about being stopped by police on Greenmount Avenue in the early seventies when he was a graduate writing student at Johns Hopkins University. He was held because he didn't have an ID, not released until an official from the school could be reached to come and vouch for him. Knowledge of Baltimore streets is rare to detect in those who aren't natives or longtime residents; his in-the-trenches standoffs filled the crowd with gratitude.

I didn't spend much time thinking about that experience once it was over. It wasn't the first and would be far from the last time I sat in a small club watching Pop and my mother entertain crowds with covers of jazz and soul classics. In reality, for most of my adolescence, I didn't draw any considerable pride from being exposed to this form of creativity through my family, because what they were doing felt like a hobby more than a necessary tool for self-expression. My perception of artistry—specifically music—was that it could only be validated by relative wealth and widespread visibility. American popular culture implied this class-informed idea during the *MTV Cribs*-ified period of the 2000s I came of age in. Yes, my grandfather toured with one of the most influential bands in American history, but in my conscious lifetime, he drove people around and received weekly scoldings from my grandmother about how he needed to step up so her load could be lightened. My mother, while doing the occasional gig on weekend evenings, worked a state office job that she actively hated. Their bandmates were in similar situations. We lived in working-class neighborhoods like everybody else I knew. Assessing those realities, I wasn't convinced of art's benefits at the community level. But that started to change once I got into the latter half of high school and began to build a reputation for being aware of music my friends weren't yet hip to.

One day, probably in the eleventh or twelfth grade, I came home and asked my mother about the only original song she had recorded. It was called "Groovin," and she wrote the lyrics and melodies, while Pop produced it in the Aisquith Street basement back in '93. I had vague memories of it playing in the dimly lit home studio but had never heard it outside the house unless she performed. The song tells the story of her meeting a man on the street during a rainy evening, and when they lock eyes, both recognize only fate could have brought them together in this way. So, they take the opportunity to get acquainted. She's captivated by his brown skin and bright smile, and after they hang out, the chemistry is so contagious all she can do is long for another go at it. Vocally, it's in the family of her favorite singer, Phyllis Hyman, with whom she shared a deep, rich tone. By the grace of God, my mother had the song stored in an email and forwarded over to me. I loaded it up on my iPod, went to school the next day, and shared it with friends who had at least met her a few times. "This ya mother? Miss Vickie? Damn, that's hard," my homegirl Jasmine reacted. Others responded similarly, and throughout that day I periodically thought, *Damn, I guess my mother is kinda cool.* Pride started to swell in my body, and even if only subconsciously, it shifted something in me—a desire to carry that creative spirit on in some sort of way. And, through that, I started to cherish what I'd been exposed to, the memories of my early childhood resurfaced as ways to distinguish myself from others.

My first taste of life outside Baltimore lasted all of nine months. I did two semesters at Long Island University's campus in Downtown Brooklyn, not particularly engaged in the academic aspect of college. A mixture of homesickness, laziness, and a not-yet-realized sense of direction led me right back down I-95 and onto the miniature, dormless grounds of the University of Baltimore, a school historically designed for working adults to earn credits after their nine-to-fives. UB was located in Mount Vernon, the midtown part of White Baltimore, where my mother worked at Scratch-n-Sniff in her early twenties. Like her, when I ended up in this bubble that the city's masterfully executed segregation had made invisible to me before, I started engaging with folks who were committed to living a life counter to the mainstream. People who performatively smoked cigarettes, obnoxiously ate vegetarian crepes, and went to see seventy-year-old movies at the art-house theater became acquaintances. I found pleasure in some of their annoying, try-hard customs, then adopted a few. Soon, I was watching Mathieu Kassovitz's *La Haine* on repeat, eating Kashi cereal, and taking trips to record stores to find unfamiliar music. Anything that'd make me seem *different.*

On a weekend trip to the Sound Garden record shop, I flipped through the names and album covers, hovering over the ones I found most interesting. Hugh Mundell albums in the rare-reggae section, Lauryn Hill's *Unplugged*, Roy Ayers's full discography. But the art for one CD commanded my attention. On it: a collage depicting a man with an aimless stare sitting alone under a psychedelic sky, surrounded by a barrage of winding shapes, all textured differently. Confusing, but in a way that all interesting art is when you're that young. It wasn't as straightforward as everything else I'd observed that day. Maybe the man was closed in by this chaos around him, or just at the height of an intense shroom trip. The image was framed by a black border in which the title read:

GIL SCOTT-HERON/BRIAN JACKSON
WINTER IN AMERICA

The name faintly struck a chord. I remembered seeing him live sometime in the distant past, when my mother still did the occasional weekend gig at one of those grown-and-sexy jazz clubs. And I knew Gil was the guy whose voice was sampled on "My Way Home," Common's solo track from Kanye's *Late Registration* album. My knowledge didn't extend much further. But in recalling the vague contours of my childhood experience and being struck by the album cover, I sensed enough of an entry point to make the purchase. I left, put the CD in my smoke-gray 2006 Nissan Altima's player, and took one of the most stimulating drives of my young adulthood.

I'd never heard someone articulate their love for us through song so masterfully—every part of us. There was deep nostalgia for a pre-awakened past, a longing for refuge from the way city life was wearing him thin. There was a hopeful look to the future, but honest skepticism around how fruitful it'd actually be. There were feelings of isolation that led to destructive behavior. There was sharp political analysis on the state of the nation, which from his assessment, was gradually collapsing. And still, he found the space to extend salutations to the folks around him. Part of *Winter in America* is discernibly informed by Gil's growing up in a post–Civil Rights Movement America, his youth spent watching his superheroes—Malcolm, Martin, Medgar—murdered in dramatic fashion. But the bulk of it translates as a diary, an uncomfortably personalized account of someone living within a crumbling infrastructure.

Art that goes inward in such a way often prompts you to interpret how it applies to your own life and the people you hold dear. I didn't realize in those initial absorptions that *Winter in America* was teaching me how to document my community with three-dimensional tenderness, striving for full understanding of how circumstances take people to places they don't necessarily want to be. Through Gil's eyes, the junkie wasn't just a junkie. The whore wasn't just a whore. The crooks weren't always finessing people just for the hell of it. And anybody that's spent a considerable amount of time with individuals fighting to get from under society's stronghold is aware of this. With the album acting as the soundscape, I thought of members of my own tribe—family, longtime friends—who had had their flesh pierced through by Baltimore's ghostly and polluted crab claws, pulling them down into the barrel to never be heard from again. I worried if what was being described of adulthood waited for me in the near future. Only destiny could align the stars in a way that would place the first Gil Scott-Heron album my mother spent considerable time with in front of her son decades later, having a similarly transformative effect.

In my adulthood, my work has afforded me the privilege to see performers on every level, from Grace Jones to Popcaan to the person who, outside of their gig, works at an indie bookstore. I've been guilty of trivializing the opening act, but there's a courage there that I'm not sure I'd have the ability to muster up if put in the same position. You're in a space where the bulk of people in attendance aren't there for you, but you can't be deterred by that truth. You have to lean into trusting what's most important: that someone gave you the platform to do what you'd do in a basement in East Baltimore after coming home from a dead-ended office job with a group of friends who just got off from their own dead-ended jobs because it gives you all a fleeting sense of freedom and purpose. Lives are transformed in those moments. Mine was, for certain. Salutations to my mother for having the gumption to be the opener that night. And salutations to Mr. Scott-Heron, who is actually dead in the physical realm now, but still achieving immortality through his proven unconditional care for those who came after him. One can only dream of having a legacy of loving your people so hard that you don't even need to be around for them to feel it.

GLORY

WAS FIRST MADE AWARE of Lupe Fiasco in the early summer of 2006 at my cousin Ryan's high school graduation party. The gathering was held at one of those banquet halls with an interior so white it feels like you might have walked into heaven's cafeteria. Black people especially love hosting at these kinds of halls because it implies that the function is either too special to have at home, or the people you're inviting ain't special enough to come into your home. I was fifteen, just finishing a turbulent tenth grade year in which I'd barely passed. Ryan, on the other hand, was a solid student and headed to Morgan State University to study engineering. Though our bond had grown over the years, our relation was distant. We met in middle school one day when he complimented me on my olive-green leather Phat Farm varsity jacket with the red wool lettering, and, through small talk (and further verification from our mothers), we realized we were kin. My great-grandmother and his grandmother were siblings, both branches of our rural Virginia family tree that split and headed one state up, only occasionally intersecting. Our cousinship was more of an effort at friendship that was being encouraged by our mothers, who were also eager to reconnect wherever they'd left off. Me and Ryan broke bread in brief instances: at the bus stop,

19

where we'd talk about music, when we'd run into each other at basketball games, or at the rare get-together that united our disjointed tribes.

I looked around at his friends at the graduation party. They were cool, but they were *different*. The fashions that teenagers in Baltimore were pulling off in 2006 were at an interesting crossroads. The majority of us were still rocking extremely baggy pants—like, size 40 waist and you only weigh 145 baggy—but the tops were getting slimmer thanks to Jim Jones's and Lil Wayne's new obsession with the artfully trashy Hollywood rockstar fits of the time. Preppy, previously lily-white brands like Hollister, Aéropostale, and Abercrombie & Fitch were starting to infiltrate the hood, too. The typical footwear bounced between Nike Boots, Rockports, Foamposites, Air Forces, and New Balance 992s. But Ryan & co. were a step forward, or a step to the side, depending on your vantage point. People at this party had Mohawks with fades on the side of their heads, checkered slip-on Vans, and jeans that actually fit. I found it flagrant, but they were confident. And it's totally possible—even likely—they were equally uninspired by me adhering to the predominant style guide.

In the space, after a couple hours passed, the older folks settled into seats, where they'd remain for the rest of the event. Ryan's guests, who were previously scattered throughout the banquet hall in small clusters, started moving toward the center. I can't remember all the music that played that day, but recalling Ryan's taste, I imagine a combination of Slum Village's "Selfish," Clipse's "Cot Damn," and Jay-Z's "Allure" made appearances to much fanfare. Yet, no reaction remotely resembled the giddiness incited at the very second Lupe Fiasco's career-launching single

"Kick, Push" queued up and began blaring through the speakers. Eyes locked from across the room, heads nodded to acknowledge a shared wisdom of something sacred, and, before we realized, the actual party had just begun. From my little corner, I spotted Ryan's two homeboys whom I'd see around Ramblewood when I was on my way to get a fresh Boosie fade from Troy at the Hillen Road Shopping Center; they were swaying their bodies back and forth while they rapped the lyrics to each other. Ryan did that thing from the nineties when people would kind of kneel down like they're about to do the jail pose, moving their hands with index fingers pointed in every direction, reciting, *Landed on his hip and bust his lip / For a week he had to talk with a lisp like thiiith.* Something about Lupe's producer Soundtrakk joining a sampled violin from the Filipino singer Celeste Legaspi's "Bolero Medley" with a simple drum pattern, as Lupe shared a story about a young man leaning into his passions, helped guide these people to a place of belonging. And while all that beauty was happening, I thought, *Man, these niggas corny as shit.*

Lupe, from what I experienced in that moment, was too counter to the Lil Wayne, Young Jeezy, Three 6 Mafia, Lil Boosie, and Gucci Mane that occupied most of the space on my homemade mixtapes for me to enjoy his music. He appeared to be the new mainstream version of college-friendly backpack rap that had been bubbling in the underground. Further, his embrace of nerd culture felt antithetical to what I typically turned to rap for: to channel an exaggerated expression of grit. The prospect of submitting to his take on rap felt like it would expose a dimension of myself I was actively suppressing. But seeing him resonate so deeply with Ryan and his guys made me jealous. They seemed free in a way that was unfamiliar to me. I wasn't ready to shed the facade of a hard exterior even though I'd only been, at best, a witness to most of the shit my favorite rappers talked about. I was getting suspended from school for avoidable violations: orchestrating a dice game that was captured on the hallway cameras nobody thought worked, cutting class to go get jerk chicken for a girl who'd never had Jamaican food, allegedly conspiring to start a riot during a pep rally. I'd held guns for friends in my locker after some older dudes pressed up on them, even though I didn't know how to use one. I was banned from a local Nordstrom after getting caught stealing True Religion jeans with my friends. And fired from my first job as a busboy at Bob Evans for stealing a customer's phone while cleaning their table. "You a dumb motherfucka" was a sentence my mother started using frequently when addressing me around this time, too fed up and exhausted to offer more. For me, none of that experience aligned with the perspective of a dude in glasses enthusiastically rapping about skateboarding. I was still in a stage of mental development that told me there was no room for duality: you were either one way, or the other.

At my core, I knew I wasn't prepared for the ultimate consequences that came from doing the shit I was flirting with, but it was so exhilarating I didn't care. Getting caught was minor, as long as I got to perform the mischievous act and brag about it afterward. It was performative American masculinity rendered through adolescent inner-city fantasy—observing and duplicating the actions of people who were rewarded with popularity and access to sex. I wanted nothing more than to be valued under those laws. But Ryan and his boys didn't appear to be experiencing those pressures. From what I could see, they didn't even have an exterior to shed. I wanted to know what it felt like to not be swayed by the outside noise, and they appeared to have already mastered the game.

Later that summer, after I realized Lupe was the skinny, apple-headed brother whose verse I really enjoyed on "Touch the Sky," I went on a LimeWire deep dive for whatever I could find of his, those scenes of joy from the graduation party looping through my mind. Piece by piece, I started to familiarize myself with assorted tracks from his three-part *Fahrenheit 1/15* mixtape series. Songs like "Knockin at the Door," "Lupe the Killer," and "Ooh" established that I'd been too quick to judge. Each was an exercise in weaving narratives of the Black American condition together in a way that was exhilarating instead of sanctimonious. References to films, geopolitics, and urban planning felt like homework I'd be glad to study, especially when combined with the fact that Lupe was just simply very good at what he did. During my research, I realized "Kick, Push" was a mainstream play, but it wasn't really reflective of what was at the core of Lupe's music. He had songs that shouted out his block, Madison Street, on the West Side of Chicago and said, "Fuck the police," but he also had songs about trying to be a good Muslim. He comprehensively unpacked how children from his neighborhood, facing a string of disappointments from everyone close to them, would turn to the street for relief. That panoramic appraisal of the hood, compounded with his love for Ice Cream sneakers, Junya Watanabe, and other one-off articles of high fashion, framed him as a paradoxical figure in a similar way as that other dude from Chicago with the wired jaw who came a couple years prior. But, unlike that guy, Lupe's contradictions drew inspiration from somewhere other than a desire to be an immovable force in pop culture. It started to feel like I'd found a rapper whose experiences actually mirrored how I was starting to see the world—or better yet, someone who placed the proper language to how I had already been seeing it.

Lupe was a key force in adding another, much-needed layer to the caricature-level, larger-than-life 2000s rap canon. Acts like him, Kid Cudi, the Cool Kids, the Pack, and Wale started to kick the door down after Kanye cleared the way with raps that embraced more vulnerability than most were used to. They projected images that were more indicative of schoolkids who hung out at malls than on the streets. Their truth was paramount in contextualizing the straight Black American male experience from a more three-dimensional view.

The mythology, especially during that era, was that everybody around the way is a street nigga-in-training—a clone popping out of a self-replicating vortex with no disparity among them. This bogeyman narrative, old as African people's arrival to this country, has done our people a disservice, straightening our curves and skewing our realities, framing us as more one-note than we could ever be. When I grew up, there were complete nerds on my block—playing-Yu-Gi-Oh!-on-the-porch-every-day kind of nerds. Some of those nerds had siblings that played the streets. There were class conflicts in the hood between the elders who were homeowners and the younger families who arrived from even worse hoods. There were people in the hood who successfully towed the line of hanging with the gangstas, but staying out of the way when actual gangsta shit went down. There were people in the hood who called the police on their neighbors at the slightest inconvenience. I don't think Lupe successfully spoke for all of these characters, but you could feel that he was frustrated by the forced rigidity of our public-facing image and what consuming that lie was doing to us.

I knew deep down I was more complex than I led on, but could not bring myself to refuse those lies without someone else—braver than I—leading the way. Partaking in mischief was a genuine passion of mine, but it was also good PR for my survival. What wasn't good for my PR were the many Sundays I spent in church because I wasn't given a choice otherwise; or how, for much of my middle school years, I attended a before-care program because my father was concerned for my safety in catching the bus from East Baltimore to the only public school in the uppity, old-money Roland Park neighborhood; or that I knew just as much music by Usher, Brandy, and Carl Thomas as I knew the hard shit. When surveying the playing field around me, those facts felt better hidden than shared.

I look at "Glory" from Lupe's 2006 mixtape, *Fahrenheit 1/15 Part II: Revenge of the Nerds* as the perfect articulation of this discontentment. With a doubly wistful and luxurious delivery, Opal Staples opens the track asking, "Wherefore does my glory gone?" Lupe spends each of his three verses condensing what we spend our lives trying to figure out into bite-size answers. How do we, as a people, not only identify the ways in which we're being stripped of our human birthright, but also combat being used as tools of our own demise? How, as a community, can we honor the bravery of ancestors who laid down their lives in an attempt to liberate us? How do we remain steadfast in an uphill battle that often feels impossible to win? To this day, those charges rattle my core.

Lupe put a scope on how these blows to the spirit affected hip-hop and the communities it came from, but in his assertions, he also ensured us that we have the ability to reach our full potential if we can maintain focus. The song awakened every node in a curious mind.

For the following year, I tried spreading the gospel of Lupe to anyone who was willing to settle into an empty spot in the pews. Most of my homeboys playfully clowned me for it, which actually helped me gain an even more personal relationship with the material. "That nigga nice, but I'm not tryna think when I listen to music," my man Marvin, with whom I spent plenty time with riding around the city in his Buick LeSabre listening to Wayne, Jeezy, and Gucci, told me one day after I pleaded with him to reconsider. What he didn't realize was that I wasn't trying to make him think more than I was trying to make him feel. Feel what it was like to view our world through a different angle. To get some tips on how to navigate emotions in a healthier manner. And I wasn't advocating from a high horse—I viewed myself as a work in progress, happy to be in the throes of transformation. But evangelism is a tall task.

Quote, unquote "conscious music" had a stench on it long before we'd even reached teenage years. Before 50 Cent distilled it into a title representative of a generation, the getting-rich, even-if-you-die-in-the-pursuit-of-unfathomable-heights ethos, was mainstream hip-hop's prevailing attitude for as long as I was a sentient human. Common's mid-2000s career resurgence, with assistance from Kanye's production, made some headway for a new, refined wave of everyman rap, but my mother listened to him. Same with Mos Def (now Yasiin Bey) and Talib Kweli. Little Brother hadn't made their way to anyone I knew. What made Lupe intriguing enough for me to embrace his messaging was that he was just young enough to be relatable. In my sixteen-year-old mind, someone wearing a Bape hoodie and expensive Japanese denim, yet who still called to weigh in on the dysfunctions of our community and was forthright in his music about loving women, all while letting muhfuckas know they could never outrap him, was someone worth listening to. And I did more than just listen—I indoctrinated myself in everything he had going on. Even with all the other music that occupied my time, none felt as purposeful or gratifying as his did.

Thankfully for me, the cosmos did their cosmic thing, and Lupe ended up on the bill for 2007's Artscape, a huge free annual outdoor arts and music festival that happens in Central Baltimore every summer. I alerted every person I knew who shared admiration for his work and made sure to be there in time to at least get a view from the top of the grassy hill that looked down on the main stage. By then, his mainstream debut, *Lupe Fiasco's Food & Liquor*, had been out for nearly a year, and his reach had widened significantly. But the bulk of people I knew still had the same impression of him that I initially did—letting his first single define the totality of his artistry.

He performed the expected tracks such as "Kick, Push" and "Daydreamin'," but he also squeezed in deep cuts from the *Fahrenheit* tapes like "Switch (The Science Project)," a take on the beat from Mike Jones's "Still Tippin.'" Instead of following the leads of

Jones, Paul Wall, and Slim Thug and jubilating about how he contributes to his city's culture, he conducted a lyrical experiment that required him to change his flow and subject matter every four bars. Each pivot honored stylistic approaches from the East Coast, South, and Midwest, ultimately presenting a comprehensive guide to the many approaches to hip-hop. Watching him perform, I was swept up in the unexpected dexterity he brought to a track that I had previously (and gleefully) associated with curvy women dancing to in the original song's video. But in my little corner of the venue, not many others seemed enthused or even aware of what they were hearing outside of what played on the radio.

As I look back, that Artscape may well have been the first time I caught a live performance from an artist I really wanted to see. There's a loneliness in being pumped up on anticipation for something that everyone else is indifferent toward. Most people weren't necessarily there for Lupe; Keyshia Cole was the headlining act that year, and folks were waiting around for Lupe's set to end so hers could begin. But as I looked around that grassy hill, I did spot a few others who shared my enthusiasm. Maybe it wasn't their outward energy that gave them away; it was more detectable in their attentive gazes and proud grins that revealed they were experiencing a sense of belonging in those moments, too. The night ended with the crowd collectively harmonizing to Keyshia's "I Should Have Cheated" and "Love," and I headed home elated.

About six months later, the opportunity to experience Lupe on a stage specifically dedicated to him presented itself when he was billed to play at the now-closed Club Sonar downtown. The prospect of being in a space where I could be one of many bellowing out every lyric until my throat got scratchy was euphoric. It was January of 2008. I was a senior in high school and, by this point, a scholar on all things Lupe. I'd listened to every song of his that I could find through the depths of the internet. "Sunshine" became my go-to when I was trying to tell a girl how much I liked her—I tried it on multiple. "Failure" made it feel like I possessed something within me that could shake the earth if I wanted. I listened to "The Cool" to affirm the daydreamer in me, whose best moments were in solitude thinking of ways my immediate world could be altered by supernatural forces.

The hard exterior I was trying to preserve when I'd first encountered Lupe's music at Ryan's party nearly two years before softened, and as a result, my friend group gradually diversified. It's not that I didn't hang out anymore with my friends that I shot dice, smoked blunts, and took joyrides with; those were some of my closest bonds. But I started balancing that out by befriending people who rarely got in trouble and didn't participate in who-fucked-more-girls-this-school-year competitions. People I felt less pressure to impress. These new friends also didn't need convincing to fuck with Lupe's music. The difference between them and Ryan's crew was that Ryan's crew not only connected to the material, they also took pride in having recognized its appeal early on. My new buddies were equally swept up by his skill and potential pop star promise.

Lupe Fiasco's The Cool, his sophomore album, came out a month before the Baltimore show. I went to school late that day so I could go to Target and buy the CD, go back home, upload the album to iTunes, and put it on my iPod. In the weeks following its release, I bombarded enough friends with the music that they caved in and became fanatics. The album was supposed to follow a central theme inspired by a track titled "The Cool" on *Food & Liquor* in which Lupe built a narrative around three comic-like characters (The Cool, The Streets, The Game) who represented different stages of a man's life who lost himself chasing money and fame on big-city boulevards. It didn't necessarily achieve that in totality on the record, but in the abbreviated moments where he was successful, it was deliciously effective: a prequal to "The Cool" that explains the man's obsession with street life; a song describing a virus of some sort that's threatening humanity (which feels like a metaphor for the temptation to self-destruct); another where he personifies the social ills that keep people in disadvantaged positions they'll likely never escape. I got the sense that, as an artist, he took personal improvement seriously, and through *The Cool*, I felt like I was growing along with him—sharper on identifying what was wrong in the world. After weeks of absorbing it, I needed a considerable amount of people down to roll to the show with me to ensure a night that'd be cemented in our shared psyches.

On the night of the show, I was the last person my homeboys picked up. We were five deep—Aaron (or Urn, if you're from Maryland), Kyle, Miles, myself, and Dennis behind the wheel. A car filled with our homegirls Troy, Aseelah, and some others I can't remember was trailing. I finessed the passenger seat in Dennis's coupe and looked back at everybody else, surveying their fits. "Boy, ya feet long as shit in the back seat," I threw back to Urn, and the car erupted with laughter. We turned off my street in Northeast Baltimore, right around the corner from Morgan State University, and started to head down Perring (or, Purn) Parkway. We were going fast, but not in a particularly reckless way. As Dennis pushed down the road, we hurled more insults at one another in good faith. Threw some Pringles back and forth. Ahead, a car came to a stop sign at one of the side streets off the main road. They hesitated a bit as if they were going to fully stop, but as we got closer, they darted out at the last minute. Then time got really slow.

The last thing I remember from that drive was a thunderous *BOOM*. When I regained consciousness, I realized we'd spun around multiple times. The car was totaled. Instinctually, I hopped out, ran over to the median strip, and sat on the ground against a gate. The hours I spent playing *Grand Theft Auto: San Andreas* led me to believe that all cars catch on fire and explode when they crash. Friends from the trailing whip came up to me, visibly shaken up. "Lawrence . . . Lawrence! Are you okay? Somebody is coming." I figured I must've looked bad. I touched my face and looked down to a bloody hand. My right eye was shut.

My father darted across town from his place in Woodlawn to pick me up and rush me to the emergency room at Good Samaritan to avoid ambulance fees. Soon after, my mother showed up. Sitting in a doctor's chair under intense fluorescent lights with everyone around me terrified, the only thing I could think of was the fucked-up reality of my missing Lupe's show. My favorite rapper in the world, the guy who helped me see the light, and the only concert that I had ever cared to attend were all snatched away in seconds. I tried my hardest to convince my parents and hospital staff to still let me go—I could deal with the medical shit the morning after!—but they kept me until the middle of the night, administering eye drops.

For the next couple weeks, I still couldn't open my right eye. The doctor gave me an eye patch, and in between my visits with specialists, girls from my high school came over and sat on the edge of my bed with snacks and get-well-soon cards while we watched movies like *Prison Song*, which came on BET so much that I could probably still recite most of the lines. I returned to school like a war vet. I'd take my patch off to show people my barely opened eye, which had been bloodshot red for weeks. "Ooh, your eye is so sexy like that. You look dangerous," Kiara from Cherry Hill told me in the cafeteria line while we waited for half-cooked chicken nuggets.

When results from the scans and tests came back, I learned that the retina in my right eye was permanently damaged from the airbag meeting my face, and that I would be mostly blind in that eye for the rest of my life. It crushed my mother and father more than it did me—I guess, from their vantage points, it indicated a flaw in their parenting. To this day, when I cover my left eye—the good eye—there's still a huge black circle covering whatever I focus my sight on. It also doesn't react to light, so I can stare directly into the sun with no real consequence: a real-life X-Men mutant origin story.

I've mostly fallen out of love with Lupe Fiasco's music in my adult life. The paradoxes that drew me to him mostly started to level themselves out over time. His mastery of the craft has only gotten stronger, but the style and flair that made me listen gradually faded away. He had a highly publicized dispute with his label at the top of the 2010s for shelving his third studio album, *Lasers*. And then when they finally released the album, it was unbelievably disappointing, effectively throwing him off the smear-free trajectory he had been on. It's what comes with being a trailblazer, taking the licks so those who follow don't experience the same kickback. He's an academic advocate for the art form now, teaching courses at Ivy League institutions and releasing albums that have triple meanings, periodically coming to social media to remind us that, when judged by the core principles of rhyming, he's still untouchable. The closest we've gotten to him since is the short, thoughtful brother from Compton who's been a bit more successful at joining genuine coolness and undeniable hits with addressing our uncomfortable truths.

It was only by the power of the Most High that fourteen years after my accident, while scrolling through Instagram stories, I saw a friend selling a ticket to see Lupe perform the entirety of *The Cool* at DC's Howard Theatre for the album's fifteen-year anniversary. During the forty-five minute trek from Baltimore to the District—on a dark road that was hard to navigate because of the blind spot I earned from the last time I tried seeing him perform—I was able to reflect on my relationship to the man's music. On what it means that, through my fandom for him, I was physically and philosophically thrust into unchartered waters. For the few seconds that I went from being a carefree, joke-cracking, Pringles-tossing teen to almost flying through a windshield, I faced the absoluteness of my mortality. And, in my case, it wasn't a slow highlight reel of my entire existence flashing before me. It was instant, painless darkness that came into focus. And when I rose from it, nothing that had held me back before mattered nearly as much. Not proving that I was hard to people who didn't care one way or another. Not fear of the unknown. And not refusing myself the permission to evolve.

It took me losing half my eyesight and a decade more of living to finally see that, during the summer in '06, it wasn't that Ryan or his light-skin, Mohawk-having comrades didn't also have an exterior to shed or their own unhealthy relationships with masculinity. They just had a wide enough sliver of freedom to allow them to go where they were loved and affirmed most. It may have taken me a bit longer to land in a place where I felt that kind of reassurance, but gladly, on the other side of that, I was finally making it to a Lupe show unscathed.

MY KING, MY FATHER

A PERSON I DON'T REMEMBER too well asked me that as we passed each other in the hallways of Baltimore City College High. This was the fall of 2005, the beginning of my sophomore year, and the song he was referencing belonged to Three 6 Mafia, rap's greatest group east of the Mississippi if it was left up to me. I'd built a reputation in those hallways, lunchrooms, and communal dice games for being a connoisseur of everything associated with the Memphis act. I didn't just know the music word for word; I could recite every album skit without missing a beat. I could list off the names of their nonrapping homeboys such as Gangsta Fred and Big Triece. And I didn't stop at the group albums. I listened to every affiliate's solo projects, too: Lil Wyte, Frayser Boy, Chrome, La Chat, Project Pat, of course. So, to be asked if I knew what was being said in a single that was getting played on local radio nonstop and likely facilitating the group's real break into the mainstream felt like an affront to my expertise. I replied, "Yeah, what you mean?" The dude's expression implied a miscalculation on my end.

"Naw, yo, did you hear what they saying in the background of the chorus?" He was talking about the indecipherable melody happening behind Juicy J's "I gotta stay fly-uh-uh-ah-uh-ah-uh-ah-ahhhh," which, in my listening up to that point, felt like tonal decoration rather than something worth decoding. "They saying, 'Lucifer, you're my king. You're my father!' Listen to that shit again," he urged. I brushed it off partly because, at the moment, I had no space for unsubstantiated rap conspiracy theories. The last one that had any real traction orbited around 2Pac warning fans of his eventual demise on "Bomb First" by supposedly whispering, "Suge shot me," before the beat dropped. Even in knowing that wasn't true, the absurdity was entertaining enough to help the rumor spread. I wasn't sure if the tip about Three 6's alleged demonic exaltation had the same potential. But the idea stuck with me through the rest of that day. On the way home, I booted up my iPod Nano to investigate. The syllables matched up to the supposed incantation, but I ran it back a few more times just in case.

On each play, I sounded it out: LU-CI-FAH! YOU'RE MY KIII-ING! YOU'RE MY FA-THAH! The brother from earlier appeared to be correct in his assessment. "Fuck," I said to myself. "I can't listen to these niggas no more. They worshipping the devil."

At this age, the belief system I was molded within started to become increasingly disorienting. Church had been a constant fixture in my life. The one I attended—New Rehoboth Baptist, located in a former grocery store in Woodlawn after a long stint in West Baltimore on Hilton Street—was the one my mother went to as a child, which was the same one her mother went to as a child, and the same one her mother's mother settled on once she came up from the country in Virginia. The small congregation was made up of my grandmother and her seven sisters' offspring, my grandmother's cousins, their offspring, and a handful of others whose families had been members for just as long. We were rooted so deeply into the soil of that place, it felt as if it belonged to us. I'd run through the church hallways during service with my cousins, flickering lights on and off, daring to get caught; taken naps in the choir room when I was made to attend evening services; snuck extra pieces of lemon pound cake from the kitchen when nobody was paying attention. On some Saturdays, when the women had choir rehearsal, we boys played football in the parking lot with a group of men who wanted to be positive, God-fearing mentors. I'd been all but forced to become a junior deacon with my cousins Troy and Travis once I hit middle school, which meant we had to start wearing shirts and ties, rather than half-ironed polos. The front pews became our assigned seats, right under the watchful eyes of people in the pulpit and our mothers in the choir, who were now extra-keyed-in on our every move. On the best Sundays, the real deacons let us help them count the money from the collection plate. On the worst Sundays, I watched time move slowly from light to dark while I was stuck tagging along for my mother's and grandmother's salvation.

For the majority of time spent within those walls, surrounded by elders trying to secure a spot in paradise, my mandatory attendance felt like a sort of punishment. In the 2000s, when American society began gradually slipping out of Jesus's grip and into popular culture's clutch, being categorized as a Church Boy was a reputational stain. Church was for old ladies, husbands who were dragged there by their wives, men who did religion for a living, babies, and teenagers who couldn't break away from their families' supervision. I was the latter. What I didn't understand at the time was that my presence had little to do with me, and more to do with the honor it bestowed upon my grandmother to have her bloodline present before the Lord every week. That she'd traded drinking beer, smoking cigarettes on the front steps with Miss Mary from next door, and hosting occasional house parties, for a chance at eternal glory once she beat breast cancer in the mid-nineties. Heartfelt as it may have been, like much of what we do as humans, it was a performance—an exercise in the importance of projecting an image that reflected whom you wanted to be perceived as or whom you wanted to become, rather than the person you knew yourself to be in real time.

Being a Church Boy wasn't how I wanted to be perceived, and the deeper I got into my teens, the more I broke away from the possibility of being labeled as such. In high school, I traded in my junior deacon post on Sundays for extended sleep and the freedom to watch afternoon Ravens games with my grandfather; he never went to church unless it was a funeral or if they needed him to play the organ in a crunch situation. But there's only so much a child can do to escape years of conditioning. I didn't need to go to church to be aware of the cardinal sins, as emphasized by the community: being gay, entertaining Satan, and not professing your lifelong dedication to Jesus Christ. The constant warning that these infractions could lead to eternal suffering inspired an acute fear within, and an incentive to close myself off from unbridled expression. Some days, I'd ask myself or a firmer believer around me, *How do you know this is real? Why do we still suffer more than anyone else in this country if God is here to help? What if I'm not sure I believe any of it?* Other days, I'd carry guilt for having doubted its validity.

The heads-up I'd gotten from the brother at school on "Stay Fly" froze me the way it did because I was already on shaky ground in terms of faith. I'd just watched *The Passion of the Christ* with my older sister, and despite an attempt at indifference, seeing White Jesus have his flesh yanked out by a cat-o'-nine-tails drove me to tears. Around the same time, my grandmother convinced me to watch some DVD that, for its two-hour entirety, linked rap music to the satisfaction of Satan. It was so low budget I took most of it for a joke, as it teetered between sermon and documentary. The guy hosting the film, a self-described musician, went on about how Bone Thugs-n-Harmony worshipped the devil because the liner notes of one of their albums were written backward like witchcraft. He then spent another twenty minutes on how DMX and Marilyn Manson's 1998 collaboration "The Omen" was clearly the workings of Satan because a chord in its instrumental couldn't be found. His justification and aha moment was that, in the Bible, Satan was God's minister of music, so Satan could manipulate sound any way he pleased. All of this information and imagery pinged around my head when *LUCIFAH! YOU'RE MY KII-IING! YOU'RE MY FATHAH!* repeated on the "Stay Fly" hook. Was I flirting with a permanent room in hell? Reverend Wright, the pastor of New Rehoboth, offered a repeated mantra in case anyone was feeling unsure in their Christian convictions. Something to the effect of "I'd rather live my life as if God was real, then to die and find out he isn't, than to live my life as if he isn't, only to die and find out he is." I sat with "Stay Fly" for a week, playing it over and over to see if what I heard would change. It didn't. I considered where I wanted to end up if God was real, taking a long stare at my burned copy of Three 6's *Most Known Unknown* album before snapping the CD in half and throwing it away.

Digging a grave and filling it with a central source of pleasure took its toll. I didn't just start listening to Three 6 Mafia when they began getting regular video-countdown-show placement and Oscars. I was a couple years deep into my fandom by the time their big break materialized. My introduction to their bone-rattling magic happened in a cramped motel room in Meherrin, Virginia, during the summer of 2003. My whole family—all the offspring of my grandmother and her sisters—took a three-and-a-half-hour trip from Baltimore down to visit our folks who still lived on the land we came from. In that motel, my older cousins Keita, Magnus, Naaman, Trae, and Ryan set the scene with the essential accoutrements of an all-male bonding session—something I'd never witnessed before because I was always too young to hang. But I was twelve now, losing my baby look, and halfway through middle school. Finally old enough to not be turned away. Ryan carried bags of ice into the bathroom and dumped them into the sink. Naaman followed and placed bottles of Amsterdam and tall cans of Steel Reserve inside the ice to chill. Magnus hooked his PlayStation 2 up to the TV and booted *Madden 2002* up. Everybody found his seat somewhere on the two full-size beds. They broke out the weed and rolled a couple blunts out of cigarillos. Then Magnus popped in Three 6's new album, *Da Unbreakables*.

I'd heard Three 6 Mafia's music before, especially their big hits like "Sippin on Some Syrup" and "Ridin Spinners," which worked themselves into timelessness relatively quickly. But I'd never had the privilege of sitting through an entire album to get a true sense of what distinguished them from their rap peers in the early 2000s. "Y'all heard this whole shit yet?" Magnus addressed the room. "These niggas too hard." The rhetorical question, followed by the stamp of approval is one of the more foolproof tactics when vying for your loved ones' undivided attention in a session. Within moments of throwing the inquiry out there, you'll either see a gradual nodding of heads and squinting of eyes, verifying your assertion. Or, you'll get speculative looks scanning the room in confusion, a nonverbal thumbs-down from the audience. Magnus received the former once the album got going. It started with the ominous "They Bout to Find Yo Body," a story in which the premise is made clear from its title: *If you keep fucking with me, your mammy, your pops, the informants, police, ambulance, the morgue, and whoever else will all be dealing with your lifeless corpse.* Juicy J and DJ Paul, the masterminds behind Three 6's sound, sampled the eerie synths from the beginning of Michael Jackson's "Smooth Criminal" for dramatic effect. "Fuck That Shit" came out of the gate angry and ready to take confrontation head-on—a quintessential crunk record made for the sole purpose of activating bottled-up rage. "Bin Laden" was their obligatory tribute to weed's transformative qualities, its relevance bolstered by the smoke clouds winding through the motel room. Project Pat illustrated a step-by-step crime thriller on "Try Somethin," stretching and contorting syllables to tell a story about his desperate decision to rob a dude outside a strip club—with no mask—while the brother was taking a piss. Something different, more texturally dynamic, was happening at every turn.

I left out of that session a different LB than I was before entering. For the first time in my young life, I finally felt like I was one of the guys, rather than the baby cousin who was relegated to tagging along with the old people. Three 6 Mafia soundtracking that moment earned them my unwavering fandom. Not just because I loved the way Juicy J used his gruff tone to drive a point home, or how La Chat and Gangsta Boo were more convincing as enforcers than most dudes who've ever picked up a mic, or even that their production effectively captured their fascination with the horror genre. It's because getting lost in their universe carried me closer to what I perceived as freedom. Freedom of expression, but also freedom to make space for my own curiosities without the looming threat of authoritative interference. And, for that, I spent many waking hours delving into as much of the group's story and discography as I could access.

The lore starts here: On Halloween 1989, a pair of teenage brothers from South Memphis vowed to start taking the craft of rapping seriously. The younger of the two, Paul, had been taking piano lessons for a year. Ricky, two years older, was playing bass and electric guitar, probably influenced by the effortless cool that seeped out of everything Prince put out. But they wanted to partake in the newest Black-led musical trend sweeping across the nation, especially the brash, fuck-whoever-don't-like-it brand of rap coming out of Los Angeles and fronted by NWA. Paul and Ricky had always bonded over a shared obsession with horror films (*The Texas Chain Saw Massacre*, *Friday the 13th*, *Halloween*), and what better day for the coronation of their next chapter in life than the one that provided the most sustenance for their dark imaginations. They landed on Da Serial Killaz for a name, setting themselves on an early track of theatric, gory shock value. NWA instilled fear and paranoia in White America and concerned Black parents just by amplifying shit that was close to reality, if not fully true. But unchartered territory awaited kids whose obscenities could be drawn from bloodthirsty fictional storylines, mixed with their experiences growing up in a hot spot of the urban South.

Da Serial Killaz first tape was made by the end of that school year, with Paul—simply going by DJ Paul—handling production and Ricky, going by Lord Infamous, handling the majority of songwriting and vocals. Legend has it that the syrupy, hypnotizing triple-time flow Lord is infamous for would take hold of him like a possession whenever it was time to rap, the same way jazz singers scat, moved by the spirit more than following a predetermined script. They sold the tapes at school for $4 a pop and their popularity started to spread throughout their side of town. Soon they were in high demand at hole-in-the-wall parties. At the same time in North Memphis, another teenager named Jordan was clearing a similar path by making beats, rapping, and DJing at parties under the name Juicy J. Aware of each other from how their names were ringing bells on the party circuit, in one way or another Paul and Juice crossed paths and became fast friends, teaching each other different tricks and methods for beat-making. With them producing and Lord on the mic, they formed a trio called Backyard Posse that established the building blocks of their sinister, creeping brand of street music.

Somewhere down the line, while still in their teens, the three linked up with Koopsta Knicca, who went to high school with Paul first before being kicked out and ending up at the same school as Juice. According to an old Koopsta interview, he and his mother suffered an ungodly amount of physical abuse from his stepfather, sending him down an angry, violent path and various stints in group homes. When he finally escaped a home up in Knoxville and found his way back to Memphis, he started to hang out with

Backyard Posse regularly. Koopsta rapped in a similar triple-time pattern as Lord but in a hushed, almost whisper-like tone, adding a harrowing new layer to the group's existing sound. Paul, Juice, and Lord recognized Koopsta's contributions as something that could provide a fullness to what they'd already been making. So after some fine-tuning as a unit, the four collectively birthed the Triple Six Mafia.

What linked them together is that they all shared an underdog mentality. People doubted Paul's DJing ability because he dealt with Erb's palsy, a condition that led to his right arm not fully developing; Koopsta was suffering from self-esteem issues related to abuse he endured; Juice and Lord had their own crosses to bear. So, while horror films played a role in shaping their ominous and often-demented music, so, too, did their experiences. You don't get a group of young people advocating for their audience to brawl with one another or radiating glee over indiscriminately shooting folks without a genuine amount of rage. Because, inside everyone, there is a burning desire to purge. That is the foundation from which they branched out.

The best musical groups have a multipronged mythology to them. Origin stories are murky; some essential information will overlap, or not, depending on who offers it. Which member we enjoy the most often dictates whose memory we ascribe validity to. Some say Lord Infamous is responsible for the group's demonic leanings. We know he inspired its name after describing them as "the Triple Six Mafia" in a rap and it stuck. Most don't credit Koopsta with innovating much of anything within the group. Some say South and North Memphis would never have gotten on the same page had Triple Six's members not facilitated their

respective hoods unifying for the cause of establishing a formidable scene—if you count packing tight, smoke-filled dance
floors to throw elbows and beat the hell out of one another while
booted up off the powder as unifying. What is for certain is that,
when those initial four finally assembled and put a name on it,
they emerged as something that had never been seen in hip-hop:
gothic Black Southern representatives of Generation X who drew
from the same ancestor-informed mysticism that Toni Morrison
used to raise Sethe's baby back from the dead.

For the rest of the nineties, the Triple Six Mafia's family dou-
bled in size if you count the two official members they added
with Crunchy Black and Gangsta Boo, plus the ongoing affiliates
who, in most people's eyes, were just as crucial: Project Pat, La
Chat, M.C. Mack, T-Rock, and Kingpin Skinny Pimp. They honed
in on a detectable sound with crispy snares that skip then roll,
hi-hats that tick, strings that cry, bass that hums, sadistic keys,
and sampled vocals from their own songs that are distorted
enough to sound like wicked conjuring. Their breakthrough came
at a moment when there was an outpouring of music from the
South; the rest of the country was finally familiarizing itself with
what came from Black Americans' home base. "Sippin on Some
Syrup" became inescapable during the summer of 2000. Their sin-
gles were the extent of my knowledge until I sat in that room in
Meherrin, Virginia, three years later.

Whenever I listened to Three Six, I felt the catharsis they aimed
to inspire. But it was their visual identity that enchanted me, how
they built into this lore of debaucherous and scary supernatural
engagement. Early album covers featured them in haunting black
masks; some depicted them simulating crucifixion, while others

had animations of lightning striking down on scattered skulls. Their album titles read like chapters of an ongoing Armageddon: *The End*, *Chapter 2: World Domination*, *CrazynNDaLazDayz*, *When the Smoke Clears*. Their record label, Hypnotize Minds, channeled a similarly dark aesthetic, its logo the grim reaper swinging a clock back and forth. I was captivated by how taboo it all felt, and since they never pledged allegiance to the devil outright, there was still a moral escape route for me, if ever needed.

Around the time "Stay Fly" dropped, I was in my final days of regular church attendance. Those times I did show up—usually out of internal guilt or being actively guilted by family—I developed a ritual. I would come into New Rehoboth, find a seat in one of the back rows, grab a Bible from the nook in front of me, and immediately flip to its last chapter, the book of Revelation. Whatever was happening during service was of no interest. Whether a sermon was being delivered or a tearful testimony grabbed the room, I would carefully scan those pages, enthralled by the theatrics of a disobedient world being brought to its knees. Creatures with lion bodies and eagle wings, debilitating earthquakes, an Antichrist deceiving the world; the sounding of trumpets before cataclysmic storms. The fantastical depictions of chaos kept my attention more than anything being acted out in front of me.

Looking back with adult eyes, I recognize how much of Three 6 Mafia's artistic output was born out of a similar fixation with the contents of Revelation, at least indirectly; Juicy J and Project Pat's dad was a preacher in Memphis, and it feels safe to assume that had some influence on them going in the opposite direction. Their Hypnotized universe's imagining of powerful storms; the corpses present in album artwork; Lord Infamous listing off 2000s-era pathogens like West Nile in "They Bout to Find Yo Body"; and the decadent lifestyle they profess to are all attempts to reveal aspects of the Christian story that are too often glossed over or neglected. Three 6 replaced fearmongering with full-bodied storytelling; art that broke down the ironclad wall of fear that keeps religion strong.

The minute I started reading over-the-top tales about multi-eyed critters with wings and trumpets signaling the apocalypse, I knew I wouldn't be sticking around in the church much longer. But distancing yourself from a house of worship that's deep-rooted into your family structure has great potential for blow-back. I had to make sure the exit ran smoothly. No overzealous open-table discussions about when I began to have doubts or being manipulated into having prayers sent up in my behalf. I was still trying to figure out how to present this stance when Three 6's alleged, more overt endorsement of dark forces made me face my true convictions about religion head-on. Limbo was no longer a safe zone.

When I threw that *Most Known Unknown* CD away, I gave myself a set of rules. I would not listen to any songs that were *listed* under Three 6 Mafia. If they popped up as featured artists on another person's song, I could indulge. Project Pat, whose music was solely produced by DJ Paul and Juicy J, never left my rotation. Without fully unplugging, I wanted to give myself reasonable doubt, just in case consequences presented themselves.

Those restrictions lasted all of two weeks before their music made a full comeback into my life. I decided the risk of eternal hellfire was worth the trouble if I could have them soundtrack it. None of it mattered anyway, because where "Stay Fly" sounds like it's hailing Satan is really just backing vocals that were taken from seventies R&B singer Willie Hutch's "Tell Me Why Has Your Love Turned Cold." One of Paul and Juice's favorite sources of samples throughout the years, Hutch starts the song scatting in a rhythm that sounds like "Lucifer, you're my king. You're my father," and as the vocals become clearer, you'll hear that it repeatedly says "Tell me why," which I didn't learn until years after my crisis. I was sent down an existential path from a false alarm and, in the process, learned to let go of restrictions that no longer serve a purpose. And to revel in the possibilities of what can happen if we allow one another to dance every now and again with what we've been told to be fearful of.

A LOVE LETTER
TO STEAMED CRABS
PILED ONTO A
BED OF NEWSPAPER

A RECURRING SCENE PERSISTS IN my mind during idle time. I'm in a kitchen that resembles the one from my grandmother Bert's old house on Cliftview Avenue. A white refrigerator greets me as I step in from the rarely utilized dining room. The checkered tile starts where the crunchy burgundy carpet stops. The wobbly wooden table is always covered by a paisley cloth, which, too, is crunchy from dried-up juice spills and Cheerios bits; Bert's the neighborhood daycare lady. At the head of the table, a small television with episodes of *Judge Mablean* plays on an infinite loop. Next to the TV, a half-open backdoor lets in some early-evening breeze. Vapor from the chicken wings in Bert's cast-iron skillet wiggles its way out. Through the screen door I see the neighbors' clothes hanging on the line, flailing midair. Rival cats are vying for control of the alley, hissing at one another. One has bass in its voice. The wall phone rings and Bert, studying the caller ID, picks up. "Yeah!" Sound like my aunt Joanie coming through the receiver. In between the indistinct chatter, Bert replies:

"See if they got large females."

"How much they said?"

"Mm."

"They oughta be shamed of theyself charging people that much."

"Well go 'head and get 'em if you wanna spend that."

"Grab some newspapers, too, Joanie."

"I need the coupons out the ones I got."

Joanie, by forces of magic, immediately appears at the door and a familiar, euphoric smell starts to work its way into the kitchen. She walks in cradling a white box, while her hands grip a stack of those old supermarket newspapers. Orange limbs are protruding from the box as if they're reaching out to their new, heavenly portals. My father, my cousins Alicia and Aaron, plus Miss Linda from next door, are here now, too. Our movements start to sync instinctually. Everybody takes pieces of newspaper from Joanie's grip and carefully layers them over every inch of this little wooden table until the paisley cloth fades. Bert grabs the white box from her firstborn and dumps a small community of the Chesapeake Bay's most emblematic crustacean onto the paper.

We go in.

The collective shell- and leg-cracking creates a rhythm. Lips smacking the Old Bay–infused seasoning off fingertips add dimension to the beat, as do the knocks from wooden mallets that clunk down to secure chunks of claw meat. A drum circle if I've ever seen one. The lady on *Judge Mablean* has been putting up with bullshit from her husband, Robert Earl, for twenty years, and between the mistresses and stress, she's ready to shed the dead weight. "Where the remote? See what the number was," Bert instructs whoever has hands that aren't soiled by spices. My father, too particular to partake in the feast, flips to the Maryland Lottery's Pick 3 and Pick 4 live evening drawing. "Shit! Little Lawrence probably ain't play mine box like I told him," she groans.

I'm never at the same stage of life in these daydreams. Sometimes I'm a small child hovering around the table waiting for an adult to hand me a cluster of meat, as my picking skills have yet to develop. Sometimes I'm a reclusive teenager, halfway engaging, halfway waiting for a good moment to descend into the basement to play Aaron in *NBA Live*. At other times, I'm at my current age, so good at digging through crab carcasses that I don't even need to look away from the screen while Robert Earl stumbles through his lies. What remains the same in this recurring vision is that no one ever leaves. I never lose sight of that detail. A police siren or a text vibration in the physical world may interrupt this fantasy of fellowship, but within the scene, we keep cracking shells, laughing at others' misfortunes on the screen, cussing when our numbers don't hit, and holding each other down after a long day of performing for the strangers outside these walls; a suspended eternity where our commitment to devouring as a unit these water spiders is crucial to our spiritual well-being.

Communion in this form is customary for people raised along the Chesapeake. It's ritualistic to congregate around a bed of newspaper where crabs' steamed bodies lie stiff; to take pride in your picking craftsmanship and to shame those who need tools to do what these Murrland fingers were bred for; to grab a dozen after work because it's the first eighty-degree day of spring and you want to share the joy of longer, brighter nights with your loved ones; to take the crabs you don't eat during the impromptu feast and make soup out of them later in the week. It's also ritualistic, as with most American pleasures, to commodify a tradition that carries the consequences of a fucked-up history.

My family tree is firmly planted in this region—at least seven generations deep in southeastern Virginia, the Chesapeake's lower half, before some made it to the Maryland side of the bay. There's a hauntedness to these parts, an American ancientness that is in constant need of being acknowledged and remembered. For some, that permeates a genteel warmth of a once-existing sense of class and order. The browns, greens, and blues of English colonial architecture, swaths of farmland, and sparkle of waters along the coastal areas are, indeed, enchanting. But on the occasion that you find yourself reveling in its historical romance, as a Black person you're reminded where you would have stood in that mythologized place in time. Under the hold of chattel slavery, the forced on-land labor in these parts was primarily tobacco farming, rather than the cultivation of cotton as in the deeper South. But by the middle of the nineteenth century, the Upper South's slave economy was shifting. The land was pulverized for the tobacco trade, eventually making the crop a less lucrative endeavor. With a lessened need for forced labor on farms and with the industrialization boom, enslavers either sold people farther south, freed them, or significantly shaved their wage-less workforce down.

A consistent loophole in the institutionalized barbarism for

Black men in the antebellum period was putting in work on the same waters that carried them over to this hellscape from the edges of West and Central Africa. The shores, marshes, and ports connected to the bay gave Black watermen the chance to hunt oysters and blue crabs, as well as build ships for their white enslavers and bosses. The ultimate prize for this was a Seamen's Protection Certificate, which, beginning in 1796, started being issued to shield American maritime workers from British impressment. Subsequently, the certificate confirmed the US citizenship of anyone holding it. For a white person, this was expected: to have their humanity and personhood validated by the state. But for Black men of the same occupation, this certificate granted freedom and a heightened level of prestige years before slavery was abolished. For those still held in bondage, working on the water provided an opportunity to purchase their liberation. And right on time, as more of them got free, more white people's paranoia began to balloon.

Section 323 in the State of Maryland's Acts of 1831 was a governmental response to Black people's increasing liberation and influence. Under it, free Blacks from other states were prohibited from moving to Maryland. Religious meetings that weren't held in the presence of a white person were against the law. Selling a piece of bacon without a Caucasian's approval wasn't allowed. And free Blacks could not legally leave the state and return without permission from a white person. Then, in 1836, the Maryland General Assembly passed a law stating that all large boats had to be captained by white men, mainly to prevent chances of the enslaved escaping. Still, Blacks' role in seafaring persisted. And it's no wonder that men who were able spent most of their time on the water. Even for those who were still enslaved, casting traps for oysters and crabs or tending to the upkeep of a ship provided fleeting moments of freedom.

A young enslaved boy you might've heard of named Frederick had dreams of autonomy that were informed by his life on the Chesapeake. His move from the Eastern Shore plantations to urban bondage on the port of Fell's Point in Baltimore placed him closer to the Northern border. He recalled looking out into the bay in his 1845 autobiography, *Narrative of the Life of Frederick Douglass: An American Slave:* "Those beautiful vessels, robed in purest white, so delightful to the eye of freemen, were to me so many shrouded ghosts, to terrify and torment me with thoughts of my wretched condition. I have often, in the deep stillness of a summer's Sabbath, stood all alone upon the lofty banks of that noble bay, and traced, with saddened heart and tearful eye, the countless number of sails moving off to the mighty ocean. The sight of these always affected me powerfully." And it inspired him to imagine beyond his condition: "It cannot be that I shall live and die a slave. I will take to the water. This very bay shall yet bear me into freedom." Symbolically, his premonition was correct. When he finally did pursue his liberty, after observing the behavior of watermen before him, he knew to wear the uniform of a sailor and to borrow someone's Seamen's Protection Certificate as camouflage before boarding a train to Philadelphia. And it worked.

I write this in full consideration that I spent time living a ninety-second walk from the same port that flows into the Chesapeake Bay where Brother Frederick and a host of other ancestors whose names we don't remember plotted their trips north of the Mason-Dixon. Sometimes when I'd stroll to the store to reup on Raw papers and mango juice, I'd smell the salt water's sweetness crashing against the docks and wonder whether it was the same scent that greeted their nostrils when they looked out into an unsure future. I don't imagine that most Black people from this region spend much time thinking about that history when we dump a box of steamed crabs onto a bed of newspaper on our kitchen table or ask a waiter at a local restaurant to add a few clusters of jumbo lump crabmeat onto our burgers. I don't imagine we often consider how this creature is, in ways, indicative of our fight to liberate ourselves in this country. But our stories are inextricably linked to these beings who lay down their lives just so we can feel better about our own, even for a brief moment.

The late artist Tom Miller had a similar recurring daydream to mine, both from his own memories and from masterfully observing his native Baltimore. In 1994, he made *Maryland Crab Feast*, a work in his self-described "AfroDeco" style—a visual language wherein he painted Black people the actual color black and accentuated their complexions with flamboyant clothing and vibrant surroundings. The scene in *Maryland Crab Feast* is so close to the one from Bert's kitchen that it makes my heart flutter. A family of six sits at a square white table with yellow borders. A brother in a beater and African-printed kufi has one hand gripping a bottle—presumably beer—while the other is wrapped around the shoulder of his partner. She has a signature nineties updo, huge gold hoop earrings, and beautiful, big African lips; her hands are busy tweezing at a crab's flesh. Next to her is a toddler dangling a crab leg with juicy meat hanging out, hovering around the table like the younger version of myself in the Cliftview Avenue kitchen. Across from them is a woman wearing a white baseball cap and a floral blue dress opening her mouth to bite a thick claw. She's accompanied by a man in a green-and-white bandana and a pink Malcolm X tee, cocking his arm back with a mallet in hand. A black dog is salivating and begging someone to throw it some scraps. The Joanie in this equation is a man in a color-block collared shirt, striped shorts, and a white top hat walking toward the table. Like her, he's cradling a pot with more crabs piled to the top, prepping the next dump. Someone walking by the gathering is glaring with envy, while an orange cat sleeps on the front steps behind him. There's a music to the image; everyone is in their proper place, playing their assigned role in contributing to the fellowship. Only a deep reverence for the activity depicted could produce such potent accuracy.

When I was growing up on the Eastside of Baltimore, Miller's work was a daily fixture long before I knew his name. Diagonal from the courthouse on Harford Road and North Avenue, just a few blocks down from my elementary school, a towering mural shows a bald man sitting on what looks like a beach with a large book spread across his lap. Among the browns and tans of the buildings surrounding it, the mural's colors pop: the sand is a bright yellow, the seagulls are peach with blue beaks, the sky is pink and blue, an intimate sunset. The page open in the man's book reads, "However far the stream flows, it never forgets its source." The message is left open for interpretation, but in the context of the neighborhood where it's placed, what the mural is saying to me, as an adult, is "Because of these surroundings and your history, there is a greater power watching over and guiding you." That's what all of Miller's work says to me. In a world that often feels lonely and violent in its relentless need for us to kill ourselves in one way or another, it's a wonder that someone could pay close enough attention to let you know you are seen in your fullness.

Born in 1945 and raised in the Sandchester section of West Baltimore, Miller was a keen observer of his environment from an early age. Around seven years of age, he developed a distant admiration for a neighbor—a man who drove an MG sports car and rocked processed hair in a neighborhood where no one else's hair was processed. Some nights, a young Miller would look out his window toward the man's house, and when luck struck, he'd see the brother painting on an easel under dim lighting. Between the sharp looks, sexy whip, and unconventional lifestyle, Miller knew, from then, being an artist was his rightful path forward. He remained local, graduating from the Maryland Institute College of Art in the heart of the city and teaching there while showing work at the Baltimore Museum of Art and Maryland Art Place. In the early nineties he started being commissioned by the city to place murals in different locales: the Eastside, Cherry Hill, Northwest. He later put out a children's book filled with his AfroDeco illustrations called *Can a Coal Scuttle Fly?* about a young boy who discovers he can transform a simple old coal scuttle into art. It must have been at least semi-autobiographical because in a short profile of Miller in *The Baltimore Sun* from February 1995, the writer Wiley A. Hall finds him in his West Baltimore studio analyzing an avian-like creature he'd constructed out of a coal scuttle, kitchen stool, and other found objects. Though his murals are scattered throughout the city, in much of the writing I've found about Miller he was best known—at least in the fine arts orbit—for this decorative furniture that he assembled out of stray ideas and found objects. "It's definitely not a chicken, it's some kind of a bird," he assessed of the scuttle creation. "But then again, it's not really a bird because you never saw a bird with four feet. It's a back-and-forth kind of thing. I'm making up my mind as I go along."

The Sun paid Miller a visit because, that same month, the BMA and Maryland Art Place came together to give the forty-nine-year-old a retrospective of his career—fifty-nine works made over ten years. The show chronicled how, in the eighties, his paintings and furniture aimed to subvert racial stereotypes about Black people; bold images of full lips and watermelon slices populating the background of the scenes he crafted were a consistent tool of his during that time. As the nineties rolled around, his work became less busy, but more piercing in its effectiveness. He prioritized showing Black people joyously coexisting in their communities during a time when the prevailing image of us who lived in urban centers was criminally skewed toward the negative. But he also made more space for human interaction beyond the color line in pieces like *Summer in Baltimore*, where he showed an arabber (one of the mostly Black men selling produce and essentials by way of a horse-drawn cart) serving a racially diverse group of customers. His purview might have expanded, but his intentions of making sure his own community felt accounted for remained rock-solid.

Miller died in 2000, at fifty-five, after an eleven-year battle with AIDS, but not before immortalizing the best parts of being a Chesapeake Negro. Every maritime-related memory he plastered on the walls facing major intersections in Baltimore's Black neighborhoods honors the continuum in which we find ourselves: loving a land that is the site of our exuberance, our derailment, our longing, our sustenance, and our future. One generation after the next.

Three years before his death, Harlem's Schomburg Center for Research in Black Culture published the *St. James Guide to Black Artists*, comprising biographical information about four hundred of the world's leading Black artists from the United States, Africa, the Caribbean, and Brazil. The image selected for the cover was a black-and-white version of *Maryland Crab Feast*, stamping that its resonance spans far beyond those who've experienced the particulars of what's being depicted. But, I'd be lying if I said I didn't feel especially validated by it being chosen as representative of Black life at that point. I'm not at all convinced of the chances of an afterlife, but if fate proves me wrong, I can't imagine a better eternity than one that consists of rounding my favorite people up, day after day, congregating over a pile of steamed blue crabs. Laughing at others' misfortunes on the screen, cussing when our numbers don't hit, music loud in the speakers, a jay in my hand, drinks in our cups. Holding each other down.

TWO PILLARS

A ROUND THE TIME OBAMA took office, I spent most of my afternoons in Dennis and Izzy's room in the arid Conolly Residence Hall on Long Island University's Downtown Brooklyn campus asking myself, *What is it about French Montana that these niggas love so much?* I'd already gone through the trouble of asking members of our cohort, whose headquarters were in this thirteen-by-twenty-six rectangle, what they saw in his music, but I was behind enemy lines. Izzy was a Bronx kid who had migrated from Port-au-Prince in his preteens. Dennis was from somewhere in that Uptown vicinity. Glen was from the Mission Hill Projects in Boston's Roxbury section and spent his last two years of high school hooping for a basketball powerhouse in Jersey City. Akil was from Staten Island. Joel repped the Lower East Side. Erik was from Boston's Dorchester neighborhood. Khalid was raised twenty minutes from the school grounds. These were inhabitants of the Real East Coast who, even in the late 2000s, were still under the impression that hip-hop's having been created in their territory granted them indefinite dominion over the genre's rhythm and presentation. Never mind that a child phenom from New Orleans had grown into the form's most feared competitor at this stage. Or that Atlanta was about a half decade into innovating this thing of ours in ways that no city had since its South Bronx genesis. Or even that French Montana, a Bronx dude who was born in Morocco, had a vocal style that teetered between a forged Southern drawl and Big Apple punch lines.

In this crowd, if it was your turn to control the aux cord and you craved near-unanimous approval, any member of Dipset— even niggas whose connection to the collective was peripheral at best—passed inspection. The ability to recite an obscure Lloyd Banks verse earned you some prideful grins or, even better, earnest assistance with your performance. And if you could go to You-Tube and land somewhere around the exact time stamp in which a battle rapper from the URL channel comedically unpacked their adversary's shortcomings while gripping a shorty of Henny, your credibility stood on solid ground. Playing anything from folks raised south of Philadelphia, though, was never a wise decision. By sheer virtue of my existence, I was deployed here with the task of disrupting the homogeneity of these jam sessions.

Before the fall of '08, I wasn't particularly privy to the political implications of Black America's geography. Everywhere on earth felt far from East Baltimore. Even the Westside. But I understood New York enough to speak their language, albeit choppily. Occasional weeklong stays in Brooklyn's Crown Heights during school breaks with my uncle Derrick, an artist who moved up in his early twenties, familiarized me with how to swipe a Metro-Card with relative ease. I knew how to fold a slice of pizza with one hand to effectively eat while swaying through speeding bodies on the street. And I recognized enough names of stops along the Manhattan-bound C train route to pretend like I knew what was going on. My sister, eight years older, spent her pre-adulthood under the spell of New York's hip-hop reign, and I eavesdropped on what she rapped and sang along to in order to identify what was worthwhile. During my middle school years I snuck into her room to fiddle through CDs for field research: Jay-Z's *The Blueprint*. Total's self-titled debut. DMX's discography. A life lived atop the concrete was where I could relate to the guys in that Conolly Hall dorm, but the beat to which Baltimore bounced made it feel so much farther than the four-hour drive that separated us.

Whenever the aux at Dennis and Izzy's room found its way to me, I accepted the opportunity as a guided performance. Sharing music with people you don't know is a tacit agreement to find ways of appealing to the room's sensibilities while still steering them to places where they've yet to spend a considerable amount of time. Somewhere you know intimately. I'd cue up Yo Gotti's *I Told U So* mixtape from DJ Drama's *Gangsta Grillz* series, rapping along. Nothing more than a few head nods were reciprocated. I'd offer some Lil Boosie deep cuts from the *Bad Azz* mixtapes. In response, somebody would vacuum the oxygen out of the space with "Ain't this the 'Wipe Me Down' dude?" When Gucci Mane and OJ Da Juiceman's "Make the Trap (Aaaye)" came on back home, no one I knew could contain themselves amid DJ Supastar J. Kwik's obnoxious sirens and Juice's zapped ad-libs. But at LIU, besides some amused half smiles from Glen, the most heartened reply I got was from Akil, who, midway through one particular aux residency, stood up, grimaced, and spat, "This is *poison*. This is what y'all playing down there?"

Might as well have called me a bama.

I'd been getting subtly tried for the bulk of that first semester at LIU for my perceived otherness. One evening, after running around the city, I returned to campus and found the guys down in the cafeteria and asked what time they planned on heading to the dorms. "What. Tiiiime. Yawww niggas. Goiiinnn. Baacckk. Upstaaaas," Glen mocked. "God damn you talk slow as hell. Country-ass nigga." It took until the third time Joel held out two fingers to ask me "How many?" before I realized he was making fun of the Baltimore accent that, months prior, I'd no knowledge of having. Another time, I was hanging out with a girl in my own room talking about our schooling experiences before we got to college. "You say *ha* school, not high school." She giggled. I shrugged in annoyance. My self-perception was being dismantled as more time passed and I eventually had to ask myself, *Am I country?*

Where I was from, country as folks might have been, *country* was a slur. Despite everybody's country Grandma and that we regularly headed one state down to rural Virginia to break bread with the family we'd left behind for industrial employment generations prior, or that we filled church buses, led by our country pastor, to deeper parts of the country for fellowship. *Country*, in our Maryland minds, was reserved for people who were unaware of their perceived quirks; too free in their command of language and expression to adhere to uppity, subtle wannabe-white laws like the citified negroes had been doing since they resettled in the metropolises. But at LIU, I started to realize I was of a more hybridized, urban Upper South existence—of a people so regularly reminded of their country-ness that they develop an antagonistic denial of it. A denial I was no longer afforded in the North. To New Yorkers, anything south of Jersey is country, so they're a bit unqualified when it comes to geographical distinctions. But what I think they're getting at, culturally, when they dish out those labels is that they don't come from a culture that is informed by just the Black American experience. New York City is the world's mirror, populated by Black folks from what feels like every corner of the African diaspora. Or every diaspora, for that matter. What was brought up to their wide avenues during the Great Migration isn't as in your face as in other places in the country.

Country-ness is informed by the stories and experiences retained—physically and spiritually—from the heartland. It is often an innate way of being rather than a concerted effort. Hanging on the porch while my grandparents swung in their rocking chairs and swatted flies was my favorite childhood pastime. Buying a mouth full of golds with the first check from your part-time job (if not earnings from the dope hole) was the goal of kids in my orbit. My lackadaisical slew-footed stroll was a common mode of transportation where I came from but looked alien on fast, big-city streets. To appear enlightened I was quick to mention to my college friends that I didn't eat pork but omitted that I'd just recently stopped and had had enough Spam sandwiches, scrapple, pigs' feet, and fried fish for breakfast to hold me over until the afterlife. It's also worth noting that I had a Boosie fade during this time. The brothers from LIU either missed out on these experiences or were hiding them to fit into their public-facing reputation.

Truth is, I elected to play musical poets from Louisiana, Tennessee, and Georgia in Dennis and Izzy's room for show-and-tell because those storytellers felt the closest to home. The churchiness of it all. The jubilant vulgarity. The soft assuredness. It's what my older cousins played when they started letting me tag along in their car rides and hangout sessions—like in that Meherrin,

Virginia, motel room. It's what blared out of speakers on Ramona Avenue. It's what me and my friends rode from one end of Baltimore to the next broadcasting. I could've played a Baltimore rapper like Smash or our native club music for the guys, but the context I'd need to provide for artists so tightly insulated within a microworld felt like a burden. It's the same way that Glen could have played E. Burton, a rapper from his same projects in Boston, but instead went for Cam'ron and French Montana. You rode with whatever titans best reflected you and your hometown's self-image. I just happened to be surrounded by young men whose Mecca was outside the dorm's windows. And for as many battles as I fought on those university grounds to stand firm in my sonic associations, the ease of assimilation eventually began to caress my shoulders in the right places.

I moved back down to Baltimore the following summer with the kind of excruciating self-awareness that no teenage human is meant to possess. I wouldn't admit it to Glen, Joel, Izzy, Dennis, Khalid, Erik, or Akil at LIU, but I didn't enjoy being singled out. And I recognized the power and ease that came with being part of a cultural powerhouse while spending time in their backyard. I turned their good-faith jokes and shortsighted views of people below the Mason-Dixon back onto myself upon my return home. I tried to play up my New York City connection, acting like I was socialized there way more than I ever was. The weeklong childhood stays with my uncle in Brooklyn got multiplied by a few more weeks when telling people about my make-believe dual-city upbringing. I adopted an unsuccessful NY accent, contorting my local *ew* sounds to the pedestrian *oo*. The shame of small-townness was knocking me off my square.

Years before I reached the LIU campus, a series of DVDs circulated through barbershops, apparel stores, and shopping center parking lots in Baltimore, all loosely tied to the city's underground rap scene. *Stop Snitching*, from 2004, achieved the most notoriety and polarity because on top of having people from respected pockets of the city freestyle on camera, other subjects of the film used their brief appearances as an opportunity to out confidential police informants who were fucking up their flow in the street. Those exposed started to get hurt in real life. BPD actively opposed the film's messaging; tensions were still high from barely two years before, when a man, woman, and their five children were killed in an East Baltimore firebomb because they reported the drug trafficking in their neighborhood. Carmelo Anthony made a six-minute cameo in *Stop Snitching*, and local politicians subsequently campaigned for his punishment. *The Atlantic* even surrendered pages to its folklore with writer Jeremy Kahn reporting in 2005, "The metastasis of this culture of silence in minority communities has been facilitated by a gradual breakdown of trust in the police and the government." Its hype, while intoxicating, eventually wilted away with the passing seasons. No real winners in sight, save for our collective lust for Black-male chest-beating.

Conversely, the *Baltimore Real Talk* series added a more thoughtful slant to the local DVD ecosystem. It did the dirty work of trying to frame an aspirational scene within the landscape of a city where rap was second-in-command. Local rhymesayers, in the minds of most, were cornballs and attention whores, striving for something that just wasn't meant to happen. Truth be told, we were house music niggas raised on maniacal BPMs—light on our feet and loose in our hips. But playful, electronic reimaginings of Grandma's feel-good tunes and funny pop culture sound bites weren't getting us the kind of respect many craved for. So some people deviated and became carbon copies of rappers in New York, Atlanta, and Philadelphia, hoping to catch a buzz, denouncing club music as some goofy, borderline-gay movement that didn't properly demonstrate how hard we went. It never really worked. In '05, the second edition of *Baltimore Real Talk* brought this dilemma to the fore by featuring Tim Trees, who was already a local legend and one of the only rappers in the city to actually *sound* like a Baltimorean, from his accent to his choice to work with club music producers. The cameraman asked if Trees thought the city was gonna be the next place to blow in the hip-hop sphere. He made it plain:

"Hopefully it will, man, when niggas stop tryna sound like they from New York. And trying to sound like they from here and there. Niggas say I sound like club music, but, nigga, your shit sound like you from New York. It sound like you from down South. This is not Compton, nigga! This is East Baltimore."

What could've been processed as a jab from Trees was more of a plea, a wishful thought that, if people considered his criticism in good faith, it could lead to a unified scene with more widespread visibility than what local parameters afforded them. After his evaluation, the musical tide did start to gradually shift toward a more original aesthetic, but mostly due to the continued rise of regional rap cultures achieving brief moments of national spotlight rather than folks taking Trees's words to heart.

At the same time I reached Up Top in '08, the FMG crew rose out of the Eastside's Chapel Hill Projects, while G-Rock and his TRC outfit emerged from the Westside's Edmondson Village. Brothers in their early twenties, they answered Tim Trees's intonation by fully embracing their accents and rapping on production that mirrored the trunk-rattling bass and eerie synths that Gucci, Jeezy, Zaytoven, and Shawty Redd had introduced to the genre; a type of sound that felt natural, rather than forced. The brothers' impact was substantial locally, but, unfortunately, their ascension came in the crosshairs of a coming technological evolution, in which the old way of hustling music would become almost immediately obsolete. These artists pushed CDs at the same spots those local DVDs were being sold and participated in showcases where opportunistic promoters made wide-eyed artists sell tickets to perform. A new dawn, in which the physical grind's importance would fade, was on the horizon.

In 2012, the video for Chief Keef and Lil Reese's "I Don't Like" helped strip mainstream rap of the fluff it'd been plagued by in my youth. Its lone scene was shot in someone's kitchen. A couple pistols were passed around and dangled, gleefully. No one had on jewelry of significant value. Their drip wasn't inaccessible to the average person. And the song's central mission was to express an acute disdain for inauthenticity. Its immediate success, thanks to its shock value and a much more evolved version of social media than what FMG and G-Rock enjoyed, incentivized disenfranchised Black youth across America to tell their stories, as is—fuck waiting for a chance to look like you already made it. Baltimore took note, and quickly, because a year after Keef and his friends rose from Chicago to international stardom, rumblings of two promising brothers, barely out of their teens, started to spread through the city.

Young Moose sprouted from Down Da Hill near Northeast Market on Monument Street, a Black Baltimore landmark clasped between municipal negligence and Johns Hopkins University's expansionism. Lanky in build with scattered gold fronts and an intense glare, Young Moose's musical delivery embodied the best of our town: Unorthodox. Eccentric. Frank. All of which could be heard on "Posted," the song that put the city and its surrounding counties on notice in 2013. For a generation of Baltimoreans born in the early nineties, it drew a clear inspiration from the Baton Rouge rap that occupied many of our adolescent earphones (and my aux cord occupancy back at LIU), borrowing the beat from Lil Phat's "Cuttin Up." But the wisdom imparted within those four minutes couldn't have channeled itself through Louisiana's state capital; only a twenty-year-old from DDH was capable of this type of talk.

Pain yelped its way out of the man. He was angry at what hadn't gone his way, but was deeply in love with his community. He was hypervigilant. And his thirst to be heard seemed to border on desperation, in the best way possible. Addicts killed his grandmother in a burglary when he was fourteen, and while he was locked up at the Baby Bookings around the same time, his homeboy Shawn was murdered. The stress and resentment welcomed cigarettes into his diet. And for those gashes of the heart, he was stationed to exist outside with something on his waist that could summon you to the sky. It only added a dramatic outlaw effect that, in the song's video, Moose and the rest of his OTM (Out the Mud) unit brandished more firearms than Keef and his guys did in "Don't Like." A seismic shift was initiated in Baltimore with the offering. Never before was being *this* raw in your music incentivized by label heads and spread across a digital network of fans within minutes of being released.

Over on the Westside, Lor Scoota, aka ScootaUpNext, was giving Pennsylvania Avenue a dusting off, a hope of returning to its pinnacle—back when Billie Holiday wasn't a bronze statue bellowing out for eternity off West Lafayette Avenue, but a vessel of flesh and blood sashaying through the neighborhood jazz clubs with a burning cigarette set between her fingers. An insurmountable feat for a twenty-year-old man-child it seemed. The riots of 1968—similar to what occurred in other Black centers of Babylon the year Dr. Martin Luther King Jr. was killed—set the stage for the Pennsylvania Avenue upon which Scoota would grow. Like Lady Day, he traversed in his work the uncomfortable intersections of agony, pleasure, and struggles for power. While Moose was expanding his Eastside kingdom's territory with "Posted," Scoota dropped the generation-defining "Bird Flu."

In a this-is-how-shit-is tone, Scoota used the song as an opportunity to outline his commitment to lifting himself out of poverty with the profits from petty drug sales. Trapstar embellishments absent, he kept it one thousand and disclosed that his inventory of stimulants was barely enough to sustain a young man's life; the goal was to graduate to kilograms, where the real money was. His entry-level position on the strip didn't come with the authority he craved, but he persisted. No matter how many junkies had to have near-death experiences from his doctoring up the product, he was going to find a way out. How much more American could it get? To struggle against the weight of capitalistic demands, left with few options more accessible than extracting from the most vulnerable in your vicinity. "Bird Flu" made Scoota an instant star on the back blocks, bus stops, tinted–Honda Accord joyrides, and locker rooms, evoking the raging yearning to propel oneself into a more pleasurable existence.

Those introductions, enticing as they were promising, set the city ablaze. Moose and Scoota weren't just physically representative of Baltimore's young Black residents, with their Louis Vuitton skullies, open-face gold grins, New Balance 990s, Nike Boots, slim bubble jackets, lighter leashes and Honda Accord keys hanging off their designer belts. Their music, beyond "Posted" and "Bird Flu," held a mirror up to the city's isms with youthful vigor and fearlessness. Both recounted experiences with the juvenile justice system—a system created by the State of Maryland, which allocated more funds in Baltimore City to the creation of youth jails than public schools. "They locked me up when I was twelve, all my weed they found it / Plugged in with hella drugs, 'cause I was raised around it," Moose painted on *O.T.M 2*'s "Fuck the Police." Both artists acknowledged the city's lead-poisoning crisis in a way that underlined how it'd been normalized in the community. When Scoota rapped, "Niggas get they lead checks and act like they on top the world" on "Ain't Too Many" from his *Still in the Trenches 3* mixtape, he was offering analysis on the social effects of families winning lawsuits against landlords for their children enduring irreparable cognitive damage from lead paint—and how new money attracted acrimony. Moose was particularly sharp at confronting corrupt policing, going as far as naming a specific cop, the Eastern District's Daniel T. Hersl, for giving him grief on the regular because of the neighborhood he came from.

Four years removed from LIU, I often stared at the screen of my laptop in awe of the two's existence during the early days of their ascent. They looked and sounded like my younger cousins, the boys I rode by in my car, the kids from neighborhoods I lived in. By this time, I was hanging in Central Baltimore, throwing small music shows and publishing a blog-turned-zine called *True Laurels* that was dedicated to covering the underground Black music being made in the city and parts of the DC area. There was no shortage of talent to engage with. The 7th Floor Villains (Butch Dawson, Black Zheep DZ, OG Dutch Master, etc.) assembled guys from the East- and Westsides for an A$AP Mob–like collective that joined around-the-way flavor with downtown artsy visual references. Rome Cee, Al Great, Rickie Jacobs, and others held down the backpack-esque scene. Go DDm, Abdu Ali, TT the Artist, Matic808, and Murder Mark were taking Baltimore Club and pushing it to a more experimental future. But none of their music—and I say this with the utmost respect—had the potential to take hold of the majority and launch into boundaries outside of ours like Moose's and Scoota's. The two became sonic representations of the city's neglected class—a real-life voice put to the stories David Simon filtered through HBO for millions.

By 2014, the idea of a couple rappers from fill-in-the-blank city achieving widespread local support and capturing the intrigue of a broader audience wasn't terribly novel from a national perspective. But it was unprecedented in Baltimore. From the late eighties until the late 2000s, the foremost form of Black musical expression in the city was club music (now distinguished as Baltimore Club), a mutation of Chicago House that was cultivated in popular gay clubs and went on to dominate local radio, nightlife, and high school parties. The extent to which rap was celebrated teetered on the circles you ran in. Everybody knew the mainstream stuff from music videos. Well-known Southern acts like No Limit, Cash Money, and Three 6 Mafia fared well, just as artists from the Northeast like Cam'ron, Beanie Sigel, and Jay-Z did. But with little-to-no radio support, Baltimore rappers were relegated to a hip-hop-obsessed underground network. Even when outliers like B Rich, Comp, and Bossman did achieve professional advancements elsewhere, their music was a far cry from being embraced enough at home for a truly sustainable career. Club was King. A similar truth existed in neighboring Washington, DC, where go-go, their delightful derivative of funk, had such a hold on the city's Black majority that there was little space for a rapper to rise up locally. Wale, Tabi Bonney, and Oddisee were monumental for hip-hop on that side of the beltway in the mid-to-late 2000s but they, too, came before the tide fully shifted. It wasn't until their efforts and the influence of social media helped amplify acts like Shy Glizzy and Fat Trel in the early 2010s that go-go began taking a backseat to rap. In that regard, Moose, Scoota, and their two DC contemporaries were the first in our region to spearhead a functional hip-hop ecosystem.

I found their growing influence to be a treasure for my journalistic journey—finally, something *important* to push out into the world, I thought—but more significant, they brought me back home. In that philosophical return, I was forced to ask myself why I allowed one year of out-of-state college to threaten my sense of self. Why did I come back to Baltimore carrying the weight of shame? But that was the wrong way of looking at it. It's simply impossible to move through life without undergoing a series of existential upheavals, questioning where you fall within this boundless abyss. What I now gather is that it's easier to recoil when you're not in constant conversation—in person or telepathic—with the kind of familiar beauty that enriches you. LIU, Brooklyn, and New York City provided me plenty of inspiration, but not the kind that grew out of the same soil as me. I was in need of something that reinforced my pride—something that teased a future in which the outside world had a more complete depiction of what Black Baltimore was, instead of me trying to convince others of its allure.

But to love Moose and Scoota was to also contend with their deficiencies, to wrestle with what made them human. Moose's music left much to desire; his near-hollering rap voice was hard to endure for a full project, and on new releases he delivered bars that hardly differed from those in his best-known verses. Some of his most popular tracks ("OTM," "It's in Me," "Juicy") weren't even recorded on original production, hindering his commercial potential. Scoota, while much more polished and charismatic, was inconsistent—either producing shonuff masterpieces or forgettable throwaways. Both were incredibly sexist in their lyrics and, in some instances, endorsed physical abuse (Scoota once said he'd pistol-whip his girlfriend if he ever found her cheating). Moose's proclivity for violence came across as almost psychotic (on one song, he threatened to treat someone like a slave by tying them up and lighting them on fire). And Scoota's disregard for how drugs wrecked his clientele's lives felt dark. Their transgressions contributed to what made them so dynamic, so crucial to contend with fully. And I spent the next few years trying to contextualize their significance in my own zines, local alt weeklies, and national publications. As time went on, tragedy and triumph would reveal themselves in both stories.

Somehow, Scoota managed to get an alternate version of "Bird Flu," cleverly dedicated to the Orioles and Ravens rather than kilos of cocaine, into baseball stadium rotation. He started finding himself in studio sessions with the likes of Meek Mill, the Game, and Diddy, all of whom marveled at his representation of Baltimore's youth culture. But even in expanding his reach, Scoota recognized his power came from keeping his local ties strong. He read to elementary school classes on his side of town, filled with children who likely knew the Bird Flu dance before they were fully potty-trained. Within just a few years, his artistic approach served as a template for aspiring artists in the city.

Moose, by forces of manifestation, attracted the mentorship and endorsement of his hero Lil Boosie, who, before becoming most associated with willful bigotry in recent years, was a model for small-market rap folk heroes. Moose's music soundtracked much of the 2015 uprising spurred by Freddie Gray's death at the hands of local police. Both figures' success had a rub-off effect on the rest of the city, and, soon, rappers from every corner started to pop out, adding new voices and narratives to the terrain. Yg Teck, out of Park Heights. Lor Stackks, from Longwood. Lor Chris, representing Sandtown. Tate Kobang, from the Northeast, who got a record deal in 2015—before Moose and Scoota—by repurposing Tim Trees's local classic "Bank Roll." YGG Tay came out the gate with Future's blessing. There was legitimate reason to believe that someone might actually become a star, even if it wasn't the two who kicked things off.

Before Moose could even reap the benefits of the Boosie connection, the artistic bravery that won the city over came back to bite him. In 2014, Daniel T. Hersl, the cop that Moose called out in *O.T.M 2*'s "Fuck the Police" for foul play, launched a raid in search for a gun at a home Moose's dad owned on the Eastside. When Hersl didn't find anything, he went looking for Moose, locked him up, and had him put into the city jail just days before he was slated to open up for Boosie at the arena downtown. It was a calculated punishment. Moose would go on to fight that case for nearly two years before it was resolved—his momentum effectively derailed.

Then, on June 25, 2016, tragedy struck. After playing in a charity basketball game for anti-violence at Morgan State University, two vehicles followed Lor Scoota, sandwiching his smoke-gray Honda Accord coupe in at the intersection of Harford and Moravia Roads. Masked men hopped out, surrounding the car, and fatally shot him. He was only twenty-three years old. As it's been reported in the years following his death, his alleged killer, Cortez Mitchell, committed the murder in retaliation for his friend being shot by Scoota's friend Fred just hours before. Taking Scoota out upped the score, tenfold.

A gut punch if I ever experienced one.

At the end of that Saturday summer night, I drove my black Hyundai Sonata to the scene of the crime, frozen in grief. The agony I felt from a young, promising life lost—not even three years younger than me—drove me to tears, as did the frustration of not being surprised by the way he'd been taken away. I wept in anticipation of the dark cloud that, in response to the loss, was forming above us. Some tears that night came from a selfish place—having to accept that my hopes for this musical movement hitting the world stage were at the risk of expiring. Not even a full three years from the point his first YouTube freestyles started to circulate through the city and he shot to prominence, Lor Scoota, in his physical form, was no more.

Moose was incarcerated when that dark cloud was cast, dealing with complications of Hersl's wrath, and that his own brother had been murdered while he was away. Upon his release and extended period of home detention, his halfway house obligations resulted in an order to take a job at an embroidery and apparel shop at the ghostly Eastpoint Mall. Fans frequented the store to snap pictures with him. It was a bizarre predicament to witness—a punishment from the city that seemed to backfire. I paid him a visit there one day to interview him about the obstacles he was up against. "I ain't really doing nothing, I'm sitting behind the desk like Obama," he said, shrugging. Battered from his extended legal battle and downtrodden from his circumstances, Moose finally got a taste of vindication in 2017: Daniel T. Hersl and the rest of BPD's Gun Trace Task Force found themselves wrapped up in a federal indictment for robbing citizens, selling drugs, and committing overtime fraud. Hersl was sentenced to eighteen years in prison for his crimes, validating the accusations that Moose had been making throughout his young career against him that were ultimately ignored because Moose wasn't the image of a victim that city officials were comfortable with appeasing.

Before Scoota died and Moose was thrown off track, the two did manage to make one song together, titled "In the Streets." And it was a moment. To wrestle with whether the song was good would have been to overlook the significance of it even existing. Up to that point, it appeared that both artists existed independently of each other. Coming from different sides of town and being tasked with mounting bulletproof representations of their jurisdictions stirred up unspoken competition between them— a cat-and-mouse game of who could uphold his masculine duty to refrain from extending an olive branch. But I give thanks for them breaking through that wall because, in doing so, they set the stage for the cross-pollination that's commonplace in the current rap scene. Their collaboration and care fortified the city's musical future in ways they probably weren't aware of at the time.

From 1999 to 2002, filmmaker Liz Garbus followed the lives of Shanae Owens and Megan Jensen, two teenage girls from Baltimore City who were serving time at Thomas JS Waxter Juvenile Detention Center for Girls in Laurel, Maryland. What came of Garbus's time with them is *Girlhood*, a documentary that explores what landed the teens in Waxter, the steps they take to get back home, and how they fare once they make it out. Shanae's and Megan's experiences are representative of the spike in violent crimes committed by American teenage girls in the nineties and the subsequent rise in rates of juvenile incarceration. In showing their lives at Waxter, the film zeroed in on how these youth facilities, just as the ones for adults, seemed to do little to actually rehabilitate inmates. Waxter was nothing more or less than a good ole hellish American prison. Because of this, *Girlhood* is an unsettling watch. The film was primarily shot in vérité, giving

it an intimate day-in-the-life feel that, in the nineties, was typically employed when trying to send a Scared Straight message to
audiences. But, on the surface, it didn't feel like its purpose was
to exploit. It succeeded in humanizing two children who had, in
a number of ways, been failed by their schools, neighborhoods,
parents, and city government.

Still, it contributed to a long, aggravating trend of Baltimore's
notoriety being drawn from its association with high rates of
crime and drug usage, a continued incomplete read of the city's
Black population. It's not that what Garbus depicted was a false-
hood. By the time *Girlhood* was released, the city had recorded
three hundred or more murders in each year of the nineties and
was believed to be America's epicenter of heroin addiction. But
media has a historical tendency to obscure the root causes of
those realities. If there's a genre of moving image most associated
with the nineties, it would have to be the rise of true crime; popular media fodder for insulated families in Middle America to form
their perception of folks living in the country's urban centers. Just
by the nature of genre categorization, *Girlhood* fell within that
trend.

The circumstances that led Shanae and Megan to this point
are heartbreaking to see. Shanae mistakenly killed a girl that
was bullying her in a fit of fear-driven rage, and Megan was in
and out of trouble for small incidents that materialized into a
well-stocked rap sheet. Yet their insistence on living abundantly
is a treasure to witness, still. We see it in scenes that aren't
zoomed in on what caused their incarceration: When a surprise
party is thrown for Shanae's birthday and the girls dance, perhaps inappropriately, to Juvenile's "Back That Azz Up" (a scene

especially endearing because the song's magic has held up so strongly for over two decades that we rarely get to experience how it resonated with folks during the time it came out). We see it again in a scene when Shanae visits her family for dinner during a weekend away from the institution, demonstrating that there was a strong, loving support system for her, despite what led to her incarceration. The most important detail to keep in mind here is that these are children. When Garbus emphasizes their youth, it changes the viewer's understanding of how precious they really are: the way they tease adult staff at the facility, their seesaw of emotions, the way they nervously giggle when talking to adults.

But there is a particular moment in *Girlhood* that I can't stop revisiting. In the last twenty minutes of the film, Liz Garbus tags along with Megan and her cousin while they smoke blunts and joke about how Megan has stayed at a different house each of the eight months she's been home from Waxter. More unfortunate than funny, really, but Garbus interrupts the residential rundown and asks Megan what she'd do if granted three wishes.

"Three wishes?" Megan confirms, looking off into the street with an extended moment of silence, quieter than she'd been at any other point of the film. "I don't know. And it ain't no sense in wishing for anything. You get what I'm saying? It's all here."

The expression on Megan's face when entertaining Garbus's question implies that she's amused by being asked, either because she's experienced too much real-life shit to be bothered with the scenario, or she's so sharp for her age that she knows she's in control of her own destiny. The "It's all here" underscores an awareness of her surroundings that I interpret as meaning *Why wish for*

things that are already in my immediate vicinity, ripe enough for me
to use in ways that will yield promising results?

I come back to that answer when I think of my one year
away at college in Brooklyn, where I had not yet seen enough of
the world to know that the sense of belonging I was pining for
wouldn't be found in a thirteen-by-twenty-six rectangular dorm
room. I come back to that answer when I think of the initiative
Lor Scoota and Young Moose took to forge a path that, while not
uncharted, hadn't been fully cleared before they showed up. And
I come back at that answer when I look around and see proof of
their legacies in artists like OTR Chaz, Roddy Rackzz, Miss Kam,
Baltimore Bella, Young Don, Shordie Shordie, Lor Choc, and 448
Riq. There's immense power in the ability to circumvent obstacles
by surveying what's in front of you, nurturing it, and watching
it materialize into something that'll live beyond any of our bio-
degradable human cavities. There's even more power in keeping
that eternal knowledge harnessed to guide you when everything
else feels cloudy.

REVISITING RAMONA

THE BALTIMORE THAT EXISTS today, the one I grew up in, and the one my parents grew up in are largely similar, which is to say that, for the greater part of five decades now, the city has been perpetually pulling itself out of a hole, trying to make good on the expired promise of becoming a great American metropolis. In the seventies, during my parents' youth, the city was in transition. Domestic steel manufacturing declined rapidly, and, as a result, major employers of the city's working class such as Bethlehem Steel slowed production, reducing its workforce. Blockbusting—the practice of scaring white people into selling their homes for cheap by inspiring fear of other races moving in so the property can, then, be sold for more to the new nonwhite buyers—became prevalent. Heroin use was on the rise, especially in the Black community. The Inner Harbor was a postindustrial wasteland, but the mayor of the time, William Donald Schaefer, saw a vision in which it could be elevated into a tourist attraction with a state-of-the-art aquarium, businesses, and areas of play for children. He made good on executing that transformation by the end of his term, but, overall, life for Black occupants (who were a new majority) continued to be an orchestrated sequence of hardships that was decades in the making.

Those challenges came to a boiling point during my upbringing in the nineties and 2000s, a time when the city was dealing with further divestment in Black communities, in addition to the crack epidemic's aftermath. The number of children from my generation with hazardous levels of lead poisoning in their systems from toxic paint chips was staggering; our rates of violence always flirted with being the nation's top. Antidrug and anti-violence efforts from the political class during this time came across as distant formalities, rather than something carried out in earnest—with the exception of the city's first Black mayor, Kurt Schmoke, who pushed for the decriminalization of drugs as a potential solution.

In the last decade, while making headlines for having one of the more corrupt police forces in the country, Baltimore has experienced unprecedented levels of murder (exceeding three hundred homicides every year between 2015 and 2022)—all while city officials attempt to accelerate the prospects of gentrification. Dilapidated and vacant buildings still populate much of the place, especially in the parts where Black people live, and the handful of spots where whites whose lineages trace back to Eastern Europe, and more recently Appalachia, occupy. And, in the spring of 2024, the city's Key Bridge collapsed after being struck by a container ship, killing six maintenance crew workers. With that history in mind, the worst depictions of us have now become standard in how we're perceived by the outside world.

The city is a hard sell, from how I see it, regardless of how deep my love for the place runs. Quality of life has gradually gotten worse since the riots in 1968, activated by King's assassination. After the riots, the bulk of working-class whites grew anxious and fled to the burbs, places like Perry Hall, White Marsh, Timonium. That trend continued through my formative years. Black people from the inner city who, a generation ago, locked down careers at Social Security and other government agencies also headed to the burbs to treat their underclass PTSD and distinguish themselves with an air of self-appointed prestige; places like Randallstown, Woodlawn, and Owings Mills have become hot spots. Despite efforts to maintain out-of-state college students and lure in DC workers who want a lower cost of living than what the District offers, the population continues to shrink; it's now under six hundred thousand for the first time in my life.

The politics here often feel like a fruitless gesture of representation to satisfy the city's Black majority, while materially changing so little that the representation reads hollow and breeds contempt. In 2009, while serving as Baltimore's forty-eighth mayor, Sheila Dixon was found guilty of misdemeanor embezzlement for using gift cards intended for needy families for her own leisure. In 2020, Catherine Pugh, Baltimore's fifty-first mayor, was sentenced to three years in federal prison after being found guilty of fraud and tax evasion; she used sales from her self-published *Healthy Holly* books as leverage to fund her political campaign and personal life. Most recently, former State's Attorney Marylin Mosby was convicted of perjury and making a false mortgage application, resulting in a year of home confinement; she was already despised by many for repeatedly trying a man named Keith Davis Jr. for the murder of a security guard in 2015 with little-to-no evidence. His charges were immediately dropped by Ivan Bates as soon as he defeated Mosby in 2022's Democratic primary. In turn, these Black politicians—shifty, manipulative, and backward as all tend to be, regardless of race—are vilified to what often feels like an extreme. That's not to say white politicians on the state level aren't equally held to the fire, but within city limits, Black officials are made into mascots of a dysfunction that is perceived as inherent in our community.

Outside of a healthy number of jobs in the medical field (mainly through Johns Hopkins), few homegrown companies in Baltimore can employ enough people to turn the tide. One exception is Under Armour, which unabashedly supports the local police department and has displaced droves of longtime residents to build a corporate oasis, while simultaneously leaning on the city's Black youth to give it cultural legitimacy as a lifestyle brand. Those same Black youth, often wearing UA head to toe, squeegee car windows at congested intersections for cash to offset the consequences of the unforgiving job market. They're framed as crime-prone undesirables by both conservative and left-leaning media, seen as deterrents (or, at the least, extreme inconveniences) to white transplants who are under the assumption that the "favorable" parts of town should not be interrupted by unruly children from the ghetto. And those "favorable" parts of town feel like a different city altogether. There, the avenues are littered with sterile cafés, college-dorm-like apartment buildings, murals of woodland creatures, row houses flying the Maryland flag, cute restaurants, and a police presence that doesn't feel antagonistic.

A racialized schism permeates the atmosphere at all times. It's not that Black people who grew up here don't frequent these more manicured areas—we make up far too much of the population to be boxed out to that degree. But, in patronizing these places, we receive and accept a message that our side of the tracks aren't worth this kind of investment. When Blacks and whites do share space, there seems to be an unspoken agreement to pretend the other doesn't exist, unless they have consumed enough alcohol to let their guards down.

The rest of Maryland treats the state's only actual city like a stain on its reputation, as they're fed images of filth, murder, and drug abuse to contort their logic into believing these conditions are the fault of Baltimore's citizens rather than the repeated failures of elected officials and policymakers. After all, it is the only municipality in the state that doesn't have full control over its own police department. The state also controls Baltimore's transit authority, with the most insidious infraction being the cancellation by former Governor Larry Hogan of funding for the proposed Red Line, which would have connected the city's East- and West-sides to the more centralized areas, making it easier for residents in the majority-Black sections without cars to make it to and from work. Hogan also famously cut $36 million from the city's school budget while approving $30 million for a new youth jail. This type of meticulous gutting creates a lopsided city destined to fail, over and over. No amount of cosmopolitan aspirations that intentionally leave out the majority of the population will succeed as hoped—not clearing the murky Inner Harbor waters for people to paddle boats where enslaved Africans were once brought in via the Atlantic, not a proposed bullet train that gets down to DC in fifteen minutes, and surely not poorly placed bike lanes that aren't utilized enough for the heightened auto congestion they cause. I guess they'll get it right once they get most of the niggas out of here. That appears to be the plan.

I feel the need to, once again, emphasize that these conditions are not the fault of the Black people in this city. We all collectively suffer from the mythmaking that became a cultural export at

the turn of this century thanks, in part, to the popularity of a few
network television series—most of which I've admittedly enjoyed.
Before *Homicide: Life on the Street, The Corner,* or *The Wire,* Baltimore's public-facing image was that of a blue-collar, kitschy,
working-class white enclave, via John Waters's construction. In
contrast to how they're rendered through popular media, Baltimore's Black neighborhoods have no shortage of diversity and creativity, or illustrious legacies to stand on. People in Belair-Edison,
Northwood, Darley Park, Walbrook Junction, Park Heights, and
Edmondson Village are a conglomerate of homeowners, renters,
robbers, politicians, chefs, store clerks, office managers, trappers,
security guards, rappers, service workers, cosmetologists, educa-
tors, and more, coexisting by trial and error in a segregated micro-
cosm of American society. You'd be hard-pressed to even browse
through local publications and find an honest reflection of that
mixture. Here, the bread and butter of newspapers, magazines,
and blogs is the homicide rate, political corruption, vacant properties, and the horrifying amount of fentanyl overdoses. Well-mean-
ing (I think?), yet ignorant, white folks who flocked here for
whatever reason add insult to injury when they try to combat the
city's bad PR by displaying bumper stickers that read BALTIMORE:
ACTUALLY, I LIKE IT, not realizing this exposes how they accept
the propaganda as fact. What they really mean is *Actually, I like it,
despite how much of a hellhole it is because I stay in a part of town
that is systemically shielded from those isms.*

This drives Black Baltimoreans who are dissatisfied with that
framing to carry the burden of dispelling these myths for the honor
of our loved ones, or of doubling down on chronicling the despair,
giving an insider's look into an underworld only known on the

surface. "A lot of times, things happen in places—in the world, in America, in a state, in a town, in a city—that go unrecorded; just happens, and then it goes away and people have memories of it. And I said I'm gonna record this moment" is what Mr. Ellis, an old neighbor of mine, said to me. "You know, it's a mythology of [Black] neighborhoods and people being somehow different from any other place. I would contend that it's not different from any other place. It's the same as every other place, except the accents are just in different places." It's the type of statement that comes from a place of deeply engaging with one's community. In 2004, Ellis released a book of original photography and poetry called *Tha Bloc: Words, Photographs and Baltimore City in Black, White and Gray*, a project that, while being relatively unknown—even to people in Baltimore—criticized the city's institutional failings, honored the lives of everyday people, and immediately became an artistic North Star for me upon discovering it. It was also a portal back into one of the more crucial stretches of my existence—something only fate could be responsible for.

The first decade of my life was spent in the Coldstream-Homestead-Montebello neighborhood of East Baltimore, on the 2500 block of Aisquith Street. It was a middle-of-the-road inner-city area: 100 percent Black, row houses with porches, the MTA bus lot (that the city doesn't control) facing our back alley, and the gamut of characters you would expect from a working-class neighborhood. From what can be trusted of my early memory, the majority of households were multigenerational—grandparents and their offspring. I was blessed to be in a similar setup; my mother, sister, and I stayed with my grandparents until a house across the street became available for rent and we moved there. My grandmother's sister, Aunt Ann, lived a few doors down from us, and my cousin Trae lived around the corner on Montpelier with his mother. Early-childhood memories consist of bouncing from one house to the next on that street, having cousins visit from other parts of town, and taking my few dollars to the corner store to buy Funyuns and fart bombs to taunt the teenagers on the block. I was handled with extreme care, shielded by my sister and older cousin's protection when frolicking outside.

In 2000, when I was ten, our immediate family left Aisquith Street and headed to the Northeast side of town. My mother moved to Northwood on East Belvedere Avenue, around the corner from Morgan State University, in an area that, by look and character, felt more akin to the suburbs than the rest of the city. Its wide streets were also lined with row houses, but it was less inviting than Aisquith. Most porches had no awnings, making it less appealing to sit out and shoot the shit with neighbors. There were no corner stores, only an underwhelming shopping center with a carryout, barbershop, and Food Lion. The sense of community that came with being more compactly situated on a tight one-way city block was absent, which, in hindsight, doesn't feel like a coincidence. Living in this part of Baltimore was a virtue signal that you'd elevated beyond your around-the-way origins, that yelling across the street to a neighbor or blasting music from a stereo on the steps was no longer acceptable. Because of this, the children I encountered in that neighborhood were more sheltered and less outgoing, unless you were approved of by their families. After some observation, staying inside proved to be a better option than trying to navigate a foreign landscape.

Concurrently, my grandparents moved to Ramona Avenue in the Belair-Edison neighborhood, a block and overall area nearly identical to Aisquith Street. Around there, just about every household had kids within my age range; some I'd already known from Harford Heights Elementary. Many families had moved to the block from the projects in lower parts of East Baltimore after they were demolished. Within a year of us leaving Aisquith, I was spending the bulk of my out-the-house time on Ramona rather than East Belvedere. There was a strong sense of community, a trust that your neighbor would look after your child if you stepped away or tell you a strange man was on your porch while you were gone. And it was there that I was experiencing life in a fuller, more stimulating way.

As I entered the beginning of my teens around Ramona and gained more autonomy over my interactions, the world started to open up to me. The adolescent rush of having adult-ish experiences became an addiction. I was constantly encountering a series of firsts. I went to my first freak party across the street in Kendra and Kiara's basement, where we—a bunch of musty kids going through puberty—stood under dim lights while tape recordings of K-Swift's Baltimore Club mixes from 92Q blasted, the boys summoning up courage to go thrust their crotches behind whomever they'd been eyeing all summer. I punked out of my first mission, which was to go with a couple homeboys to an abandoned house on Dudley Avenue, bust the windows with bricks, and see what we could steal. I was too paranoid to go through with it. It's where I had my first police encounter when, one day, me, Mack, Jerrod, and a few others were in the alley throwing firecrackers into a discarded Barbie Jeep when an elder, annoyed by the noise, called the cops. They zoomed onto the block, hopped out, and instructed each of us to sit down on the curb in a single-file line with our hands behind our backs. "Who was the one setting the firecrackers off?" they asked. We looked around, kept our mouths shut, and prayed the situation wouldn't escalate. "If we get another call about y'all doing the same thing, y'all getting in the back of this car. You understand?" I don't think any of us told our families; once the fear wore off, it became a twisted source of pride that we didn't rat one another out. To this day, I'm alarmed by how customary I found the incident, even as a child—that receiving heavy-handed responses from law enforcement was all but guaranteed to me in this society. I'm willing to bet all hell would break loose if that started to happen to white children in the *Actually, I like it* parts of town.

The lighter days on Ramona were filled with a considerable amount of joy. We held neighborhood-wide tackle football games in Herring Run park—Roy would play quarterback, Mookie would run the ball, and Tyrone, already manlike in build, would just run niggas over. I borrowed Deion's trick bike to cruise around Belair Road until the psychic alarm in my head told me my grandmother was probably yelling my name from the porch. I delighted in our neighborhood tradition of using multiple extension cords from inside our homes to host video-game tournaments on the porches of whoever's parents felt like enduring the chaos of teenage noise. The more chaotic days turned into fodder for spicy gossip: the boyfriend of our neighbor two doors down smashing the window of her Ford Explorer with a brick over an argument they had earlier on; Miss Sharlene, battling alcoholism, waving a gun at me and my friends for antagonizing her, then coming to the door with a water gun when the police arrived to assert her innocence; the surreal experience of seeing someone's house raided on a quiet Sunday morning while everyone else on the block was still sleeping—cops issuing a phony warning before obliterating someone's front door with a battering ram. No matter what was happening outside, bearing witness was my top priority. I practically had to be dragged inside the house from all the festivities that went down daily.

Unfortunately for me, our time on Ramona was short-lived. Four and a half years after moving there, my grandmother informed me that she couldn't afford to keep the house and she'd have to find somewhere else to go. The news crushed me. I'd grown emotionally dependent on my community of friends. In my mind, we were gonna be like kids in the movies who start out as small children in the beginning of the film and, by the end, have grown up, experienced love in front of one another, held secrets for one another, and enter the beginning stages of adulthood as a unit. I begged my grandparents to figure out a way for us to keep the house, but it just wasn't in the cards. I imagine it crushed them much more than it did me.

In the fall of 2004, we packed up and left Belair-Edison in the rearview, and I was relegated to the pseudo-suburban prison of my mother's house in Northwood. A couple of my buddies from Ramona ended up going to my high school the following year, but interacting with them in an educational setting didn't feel the same as the familial connection we shared on the block. I felt socially cut off and stayed in touch when I could, but in a time before everyone had access to one another via cell phones and mobile apps, life naturally went on.

In the spring of 2009, while at Long Island University, I sat in my dorm room, browsing the MySpace home page on the hand-me-down MacBook my uncle had gifted me and scrolled past a forum topic that, among other words I no longer remember, read, "Ramona Avenue." A rush of nostalgic euphoria hit me in the chest. Even within the context of inner-city Baltimore knowledge, Ramona is such a small block that most people aren't aware of it unless they have some personal connection. It was posted by a dude named DeeJ, who was a year behind me in high school and was the first person I knew to successfully capture the streetwear look, which, at that point, included Bape hoodies, skinny jeans before they were acceptable in Baltimore, and vintage snapback caps. In school, we developed a respect for each other's style; I could tell he'd spent some time in New York because most of what he was rocking was only available in SoHo, and he'd started a sneaker blog that was getting real traction on the internet. I had figured that was the only thing we had in common. But when I saw his forum topic with "Ramona" in the subject, I hit him immediately. "Wassup bro, you from Ramona? That's crazy. I used to stay on the 3200 block." He typed back, "Yo forreal? I grew up on the 3300 block my whole life. We probably seen each other when we was young and didn't even know." We exchanged numbers.

When I returned to Baltimore that summer, I reached out to

DeeJ and we started to develop a friendship off our shared interests and recently discovered mutual geographical background. I drove to meet him on Ramona one day and got out of the car, looking around, feeling an intense bout of nostalgia, as well as a sort of grief for what had been lost. As we walked down the street, I saw an old friend: my man Daves who always hung with Mookie and would chill on my porch when I hosted *NBA Street* tournaments. I smiled, looked at him, and said, "Damn, I ain't seen you in forever, yo. You remember me?" He smirked back, dapped me up, and said, "C'mon, yo. Of course I remember you. You sister still be singing?" As short of an interaction as it was, I felt back at home.

I kicked it around there for a few hours, reminiscing with DeeJ as we traded childhood stories and ran names by each other to see what mutuals we had around the way. Our blocks were separated by Mannasota Avenue, and for whatever reason the 3200 and 3300 blocks didn't always converge. I knew some people from his side, as he did mine, but somehow we coexisted as neighbors throughout our early lives without ever knowing each other.

As I was leaving that day, DeeJ flagged me down before I got into my car. "I wanna show you something. Look at this." He was holding a small rectangular book with a photo of a group of young men embracing, the oldest one halfway smiling on the cover, his signature Baltimore gold fronts gleaming. The title read *Tha Bloc: Words, Photographs and Baltimore City in Black, White and Gray.* Nothing could have prepared me for what I was about to see. Inside were black-and-white photos of Ramona from the time my grandmother had the house up the block. The beautifully conjoined row houses looked like regal monuments. Memories of hopping from porch to porch settled in. Then, my old neighbors started to appear. Roy, Daves, Kelci, Tiffany, and faces of people whose names I never knew, but saw regularly. It didn't feel real. DeeJ smiled as he saw me browse in amazement, pointing out everyone I recognized. "My father made this," he said to me. "You can hold on to it."

I left with my heart filled, but also confused. *How the fuck am I not in this? And who is his father?* I thought. *Tha Bloc* was a physical manifestation of my memory, of a time I thought I'd never get back once my grandmother lost the house. Being a writing student with no real direction of how I wanted to apply my education, I studied the book religiously. Organized in four sections, photography and poetry work in tandem to make sense of Ramona Avenue, the greater Belair-Edison neighborhood, and Baltimore City as a whole. There's a dual function to it. There's so many photos that one could just focus on them by themselves, but when you read the poetry that's in between them, it's almost as if you're watching a film with captions. These images capture people living their everyday lives: getting ready for church, cradling their children, shooting dice on the porch, playing video games with extension cords coming from inside the house. The poetry, inspired by the characters you see, offers commentary on their circumstances—a reality constructed by government-sanctioned segregation.

DeeJ's father observed the conditions around him with rigor and beauty, painting a textured portrait of people who spent the majority of their time—contrary to racist framing on the news—working and making a way for their families. He showed children at play. He depicted growing boys becoming emotionally and mentally hardened before they reached high school age, toting guns. There was a tutorial on how to roll a blunt. With his poetry, he took disingenuous politicians and their shallow campaigns to task for half-heartedly placing Band-Aids over gaping wounds, like former Mayor Martin O'Malley's early-2000s BELIEVE campaign, in which billboards, trash cans, and bumper stickers promoted the word to remind residents of the Black neighborhoods that it was time to take pride in their communities instead of peddling drugs in them. (This city obviously has a decades-long affinity for the power of an ignorant bumper sticker.) *Tha Bloc* was just as much an assessment of the things wrong with American society, at large, as it was one of Belair-Edison. And it's so spot-on—equal parts uncomfortable, heartwarming, and matter-of-fact—that it makes me wish there were more articles of printed matter just like it.

Me and DeeJ got closer over the years. I was reacclimated into what was happening on Ramona, but also got to know DeeJ's father, Mr. Ellis. *Tha Bloc* had become such a guiding light for me as I started to build my own blog and zine that I felt compelled to pick Ellis's brain every chance I got. To me, someone who was this thorough in their artistry needed to be mined for information. *How did he arrive at this kind of expression? Why did he choose Belair-Edison as a place to put roots down? Was there more work he was hiding somewhere?* Mr. Ellis was raised in New Orleans and grew up in a family of prominent jazz musicians, but never picked up an instrument himself. Instead, he enlisted in the military and, when finished, enrolled in NYU as a photography student, where he met DeeJ's mother. After graduating, he knew he didn't want to stay in New York—the people in his orbit were too naive to see how the world actually worked, he says—but also had no interest

in returning to Louisiana. So he settled on Baltimore, mostly due
to its low cost of living.

When he'd found the house on Ramona Avenue in 1993, the
neighborhood was working-class white, mostly populated by
Polish immigrants and their newly American families. Only two
households, outside his, belonged to Black people. Then, a few
years later, Baltimore officials began plans to get rid of the city's
last high-rise project complex, the Flag House Courts, on the
Eastside of downtown. As families were given notice to vacate,
many started to migrate to more northern territories of the Eastside, Belair-Edison being one of the more prominent destinations.
White people started scrambling for a way out. An April 1995
headline of the *Baltimore Sun* reads, "Northeast Baltimore Neighborhood's Efforts Fail to Stop Flight to the Suburbs." The gradual
transformation inspired the early stages of what would become
Tha Bloc. "I didn't know at the time that a transition was happening other than the obvious one, but it was a lot of moving parts. I
wanted to document what was going on," Mr. Ellis told me as we
sat in his living room.

These conversations with Mr. Ellis helped me make sense of
my own existence, not just in the context of the Belair-Edison
neighborhood or Baltimore City, but in how so much of our lives
as Black people—or any people, really—are decided for us by
unseen forces. When my grandparents moved to Ramona Avenue
in the year 2000, the shift that inspired *Tha Bloc* had already been
fully set. Save for one old man we called Pops who flew the American flag from his porch and always wore a military cap and a
short-sleeved button-down shirt tucked into his trousers, there
were no white people on our block, or anywhere around the way

from what I could remember. Miss Sharlene's white husband, Jim, across the street didn't count because, for one, he was hillbilly white and had half-Black children. It wasn't until talking to Mr. Ellis that I went back and spoke about this with my family, only to learn, even though we didn't come from Flag House, we also migrated to Ramona because word was floating around the Eastside that cheap houses for Black families were popping up around Belair Road.

What *Tha Bloc* captures so eloquently is how too much attention—from policymakers and greater society—is paid to prescribing quick fixes for the deficiencies that are perceived as innate in Black urban communities, when, in reality, the goalposts for advancement are moved so frequently that people are tricked into thinking their issues lie within. "Oh, how these magic men play / fooling my people with tricks / that you can't believe / rabbits, doves, money / coming out of every sleeve / out of every hat / and out of every pocket" is how Ellis painted what he saw in my favorite poem from *Tha Bloc*, titled "my people." "Days of work reduced and worth to hours / rules changing constantly / angles changing to extend / the life of the best trick, / it is the greatest show on earth / but my people are told to play fair / and most try but many don't / and when they cheat, / they can only cheat themselves / or each other / for the hands of the magic men / are too fast." Damn.

The book isn't without flaws. Photos of children pointing guns at the camera would not go over well in these times and may have not in that time either. If nothing else, the images at least inspire discomfort, regardless of their authenticity. You'd be well within your rights to challenge Ellis choosing to show these elements of a community he wasn't born in, but you'd also have to reconcile that, when he was documenting the community, no one who was establishing this new chapter of Belair-Edison was actually *from* there. But what does being from somewhere mean anyhow? You could be from somewhere and have no interest in reckoning with a place's difficulties. You could be from somewhere and spend your days completely terrorizing it, taking from it. What I can say about Mr. Ellis is that he's a staple in his community, still living in the same house he moved to thirty years ago. He's watched people grow from kids to adults and still leaves his porch open to whoever needs a place to convene. He writes letters to people who've been in the prison system and have no prospects of getting out, the same ones he photographed through their childhood. And he does this without the promise of the project amassing any type of notoriety or accolades.

Truthfully, *Tha Block* has never gotten its just due. Mr. Ellis self-published it under a different name (Obie Joe Media, LLC) and handled distribution on his own. To this day, there are boxes of them still in his home. I once asked Ellis's next-door neighbor of twenty-plus years about the book and he stared blankly. *Tha Bloc* got a few spotlights cast on it around the time it dropped. In December of 2004, *The Sun* described Ellis as a spry forty-year-old who was "like a permanent correspondent in a half-forgotten frontier outpost." The following summer, NPR's Scott Simon joined Ellis on his Ramona Avenue porch for a conversation about the project's genesis. Photos from the book were featured in a couple shows between here, DC, and Philly. Then the attention just stopped. Not that that's uncommon for any press cycle, but, if you ask me, *Tha Bloc* isn't just any book. It's a breathing testament to lives of the people who persist in the face of redlining, budget cuts, investment being put into their children's incarceration as opposed to their education, and the fortifying of invisible borders that intend to keep the population stagnant. I fear if I don't continue to sing its praises, it'll fade into the abyss, much like Ellis felt about how the block was changing in the late nineties. The book is a master class on telling the whole story, and not just the salacious parts. Each piece of writing adds necessary context to what makes a community, and how a community continues to exist, regardless of who's watching. To strive for mastery without any proof of material benefit is how you express your love for a people, for a city, for a neighborhood, for a block. If I've been able to do even a crumb of that while accepting the role of a documentarian interested in truth, then I'm one step closer to where I want to be.

FAKE DIFFERENT

I N 2014, MICHAEL LACOUR packed his small sedan up with an
assortment of speakers that accounted for every seat except his
and began a daylong drive from his home in the Houston suburbs
to a dingy little music venue called The Crown in the heart of
Central Baltimore. When he departed, it was perfect East Texas
weather for late April, hitting the low seventies by evening. In Baltimore, where early spring brings the worst of winter along, the
high was a brisk sixty-two degrees. LaCour usually hit multiple
cities and performed at house gigs along the way to financially
sustain himself for this type of distance, but that evening, he
made an express trip this time to play at KAHLON, a bimonthly
party I hosted with my good friend Abdu Ali. This was a momen-
tous occasion because LaCour, whose stage name is B L A C K I E,
was, to us, the epitome of boundless, experimental Black music.
No one could yell louder than him, blow speakers out like him,
or use every measurable ounce of energy in their body to cry out
about society's deficiencies better than he could.

To me—a person recently finding community with people who
resided in the counterculture—B L A C K I E was a *real* Different
Nigga. He didn't appear to have any qualms about going the opposite way of the majority. Except, his path took him somewhere I

had no knowable access to. B L A C K I E's music didn't encapsulate what I understood as the traditional modes of African American expression. He made an industrial-sounding version of noise rock, which, to the extent that I'd listened to anything like it, previously computed as something I couldn't connect with, spiritually or culturally. But the unassailable presence of soul in his work was what brought me in and kept me. There was a sincerity in the delivery—that his method of accessing the blues came out as an uncontained rage, but it was blues, nonetheless. He wasn't like most of the Black people I knew who, like me, subconsciously started flocking toward alternative spaces once hipster culture crept into the mainstream. By the time B L A C K I E took that day-long drive to us in 2014, he was already close to a decade into his music career. Meaning, he'd often been the only person of African descent booked in the places he performed for almost ten years, directly interfacing with people who benefited from the systems he was trying to sonically dismantle.

Me and Abdu were trying to change that reality for the Black people in our orbit who wanted to operate on the fringes, to establish a space where they could be a little more expressive than how they were conditioned to behave. That was the impetus for KAHLON's creation. The party arrived into a DIY scene that was just transitioning out of a hipster renaissance of sorts. In a little stretch of the city's central areas, the music being played at pay-what-you-can warehouse parties and small festivals on the parking lots of vacant buildings had begun to grace the pages of *SPIN* and *Pitchfork* and get national airplay. The big dogs were white indie acts like Beach House, Animal Collective, Future Islands, and Dan Deacon. At times, that scene converged with Baltimore

Club, whose popular DJs were occasionally booked on that side of the tracks. But there was room for something new to happen as that cohort transcended local status. Within a couple years of meeting people in this scene, Abdu and I established a shared mission: to harness the magic of the city's creative community filled with brilliant misfits and transplants, while also attracting young adults from the Black neighborhoods where we were raised. We figured if we could do our part in fostering a cultural exchange, then the potential for making something memorable was endless.

B L A C K I E's music was the personification of that cultural exchange. I'd fallen in love with it a year before he came to Baltimore when he dropped *Fuck the False*, a seven-track album that changed how I listened to music, and what I listened for. On it, he utilized rage to stand in solidarity with people who were, too often, the subject of alienation and forced isolation in the DIY space. He barked phrases of affirmation into your ear until you, too, believed everyone deserved to live in a world that operated on generosity, fairness, and personal dignity. The opening track, "Girls in the Front," drops you into the chaos of a live punk show. Cymbals slice their way through, sparse basslines add emphasis, and LaCour cries out to be heard over the thrashing. From the song's outset, he clears a pathway in the male-dominated crowd for women to partake in a mosh pit without the threat of danger—a promise of protection in the space. Music with a conscience often gets the nod of approval for having pure intentions even if it doesn't inspire you to give it regular rotation, but this brother understood how to bang a listener over the head with blunt force so it'd be felt regardless. Even if that meant the message would be subsumed by the sound, the lasting impression was going to be there. In "Revolutionary Party Pt. 2," he screams, *"No time for fear"* on the hook and spits verses where he channels the great freestylers of his hometown such as Lil Keke and Slim Thug while sharing disjointed thoughts about his artistic excellence in comparison to tame mainstream puppets. But the song that solidified me as a fan was "... Is a Wasteland." If an artistic manifesto exists for him, this is it. On the song, positioned toward the end of the album, B L A C K I E's voice is noticeably hoarser here, and he raps with a palpable conviction, running through what's sitting on his heart: children being born into unfavorable circumstances, the inability to escape a destructive pattern of thinking, and the challenge of loving yourself while hating the world. It was radically honest—not just in lyrical content, but in energy exerted. Through spending time with it I gained a better understanding of abrasion—how when you want people's attention, you have to twist the levers a bit in the opposite direction to grab ahold of them.

A few months before he made it to Baltimore, I interviewed him about how the album was made. "I stayed up all night in the garage going from like nine p.m. to four a.m., sipping whiskey and energy drinks just coming off the dome. I had shit that I had written, and when I blazed through that, I started freestyling and knocked all that out," he said. "I spit ' ... Is a Wasteland' in one take. I would drop a written line, then freestyle the next. In my mind I was thinking about the Last Poets, and how they laid their shit down. That's really what I'm on right now. I don't know if it's because I just combed my Afro out or what." A futuristic soul brother rockstar, he was executing equal parts musical effort an performance art—testing the limits of his human capacity to get a message through.

At KAHLON that Thursday night at the Crown, attendance was milder than what we regularly pulled in on weekends. But for an artist who'd sharpened his sword playing for fifty-person crowds, it must've felt like home. Dressed in all black—a tee, cut-off denim shorts, and beat-up Vans—the Houstonian started his set by connecting the sound system he brought along with him. Two of the speakers, larger than most people in the space, defied the logic of their even fitting in his car. Once he got everything cooking and checked for sound, he went right into a maniacal set without an introduction. He clenched his fists, stomped his beat-up black Vans, swung his elbows, and periodically got down on his knees as his screams competed with the sonic force field he built. I watched as people—Black, white, college aged, working adults, stragglers—got swept up in his catharsis, throwing their bodies into one another or into imaginary people. Off a few free whiskey-and-Cokes and preshow blunts, I stood in the middle of the crowd nodding my head and smiling at how B L A C K I E, with the flip of a switch, could go from a soft-spoken shy person to someone who commanded such influence over people.

About fifteen minutes into his set, while the feedback from speakers screeched and he let emotions contort his body into what looked like praise dances, the electricity in the whole building blew out—turns out, the power grid wasn't prepared for the extra ammunition he came equipped with. He wiggled out of the audience's line of vision, and people talked among themselves in amazement about what had just happened. Ten minutes later he popped back up. Looking around to the crowd with a deadpan expression, he checked for sound one last time and continued where he'd left off.. No explanation, no opportunity for people to get back into the groove. The wails got louder, and the crowd went right back to collectively losing their shit. There was a valuable lesson that night: one that reminds us that, when you've earned the trust of your community, if for whatever reason you might lose your footing, rest assured, someone will be there when you recalibrate and help you get back to form. I left that show fulfilled, proud that I could keep feeding my appetite to engage with forms of our music that thrived on blurring the sonic binaries capitalism requires us to maintain to maximize commercial potential.

My entrance into this scene was more than a bit tenuous. When I returned from a year in college in Brooklyn and started attending the University of Baltimore, I abandoned the idea of attempting to duplicate the college experience I'd just enjoyed at LIU. It wasn't a traditional campus. There were no dorms, thus no interior life for me to access in the way I already did. I got a job as a salesperson at DSW, went to class, and off campus hung out with friends I'd known since high school. Within months of being back home, I had a daughter on the way, pushing me further into building a life where school and considerable time hanging out were on the periphery. I was settling into a routine that wasn't fit for a nineteen-year-old, but one easily obtained while mourning "my previous life." That minutiae carried on for months. But, one day in UB's computer lab, about a month before my daughter was born, Abdu struck up a conversation with me about blogging.

The one he ran was focused on arts and culture on a local and national scale, while mine was an unorganized stream of posts about music, new sneaker drops, and abbreviated meditations on popular sports news.

We'd known each other since high school, but rarely communicated. He came across as focused in an off-putting way. Demonstrative, ambitious, and passionate but still an inspiring energy to be around for someone like me, who felt a little listless. He was the best friend of my first girlfriend in tenth grade, friends with my older cousin Bianca, and voted the Best Dressed in our senior yearbook. But he was queer, and my still-developing manness, threatened by the possibility of being perceived as the same, resisted any meaningful engagement. After talking about our blogs in the computer lab, realizing we had a shared interest in chiming in on what was happening around us, he invited me to a party happening a few days later that he thought I might appreciate. I was hesitant at first, tussling with my fragile concept of masculinity. But I was also experiencing my last few weeks before being responsible for a human life and feeling absolutely caged in by the sameness of my day-to-day. Something to get that reality off my mind—and to confront my homophobia-informed hesitation—was needed.

When I showed up later that week, the function was taking place in what appeared to be a Gothic-looking former church. It was a mostly white crowd—the first function I'd ever been to with this racial breakdown—where all the people, even the sprinkles of Black ones I spotted, wore all black, with band T-shirts, ashy jeans, and combat boots laced extremely tight. Nondescript electronic, Baltimore Club, and punk-leaning music came out of the speakers. Little doorways were scattered throughout the space with sheets covering them; a select few partygoers came in and out. Randomly placed fog machines and LED lights added to the mystique of the space. A backdrop that read CULT with a skull and crossbones was tacked against the wall for photos. In the middle of the floor, a dude danced sensually inside a cage with no shirt on. "The fuck is going on in here," I whispered to myself. But, in the same way I sat back at my cousin Ryan's graduation party nearly a decade before and watched them bask in the pleasures of Lupe Fiasco's music before I became a willing participant, I did the same here. Except this time, it felt like I was many towns over from my comfort zone—something more exhilarating, something that no one I knew at any stage of my life (except Abdu) had access to. The dilemma was that, even if I was going to start testing the waters of a new scene, it would have to be at an incremental pace. Bigger responsibilities had command of my time. In a crowd of *real* Different Niggas, I was on the periphery; able to look the part and talk the part, but never truly feel the part.

My daughter arrived in late October of 2010. The party I hit with Abdu a couple weeks prior would be the last I experienced for a few months. I was back in a fixed routine, but with much less time to work with, it felt. Between sharing responsibilities with her mother, going to my new job as a bank teller, and attending class, I mostly stayed updated with what was going on socially through Twitter and Facebook. I'd all but retired the blog I was operating and, instead, started screen-printing T-shirts at my cousin Arvay's studio when I had free time. Every now and then, when a family member watched my daughter, I'd find my way to a party Abdu told me about or host gatherings at my cousin's studio to bring people together. Abdu was persistent in pushing me to stay active; maybe he also felt more comfortable traversing the unfamiliar scene with someone who was from the world he knew before or he needed a person to bounce ideas off of before introducing them to the wider world. We chopped it up about new music: the rise of artists like A$AP Rocky, Azealia Banks, Kendrick Lamar, Grimes, Frank Ocean, the Weeknd. Analyzed what made these artists dynamic. Were they believable? Corny? Built to last? He showed me some artful films I hadn't seen before like Isaac Julien's *Looking for Langston* and Lee Mun Wah's *Color of Fear*. Discussions followed. My cousin Ryan now ran his own blog, called *A Baltimore Love Thing*, where he offered critical analysis of what was happening in the city's hip-hop scene. I introduced him and Abdu. Together, we forged a community that was predicated on pushing one another to sharpen our creative vision. With a baby to care for, I had a new incentive to expand my worldview and my reality. The listlessness I felt when first encountering Abdu was no more. Being a bank teller became a chore, but a necessity. If I could figure out a way to spend enough of my time being around friends who were making things and absorbing the things others made, fulfillment awaited. I just had to figure out how to manage that with the fraction of free time I had compared to my contemporaries.

While I worked that out, Abdu soared in the underground. Eventually, he dropped blogging altogether and launched his own music career, creating a tripped-out, spiritually gripping take on club music that also incorporated elements of ballroom beats, punk, rap, and spoken word. I started taking blogging more seriously and founded *True Laurels*, where I would interview and critique local music artists, regardless of what subscenes they were part of. Through it, I discovered a role for me to play in this new world I found myself in. When I wasn't working my teller job or spending time with my baby daughter, I'd go to studio sessions with Abdu, serving as a soundboard for his ideas. It worked in Abdu's favor that alternative offshoots of club music were prevalent in underground queer-led spaces across the country, but especially in Baltimore, where the genre started; you might hear someone with indie-rock-leaning vocals sing over a dreamy, stripped-down club-music drum pattern. One such example was an artist who formerly went by Phoebe Jean, a beloved figure in the scene raised in the nice parts of White Baltimore who was the perfect mixture of indie and club. My first time seeing them live was at the Hippo, a now-shuttered gay club I tagged along to with Abdu. While people posted up around the club's perimeter, they stood in the center of its circular, rotating stage, wailing their heart out about holding on to a fading love in their beautiful song, "Day Is Gone."

With Abdu making his own music and me covering the music being made around us, our roles were established. He was the social magnet, an extrovert whose new musical ambitions required him to be out in front. I chose—instinctively, it seems—something that gave me the flexibility to perform the job whether people saw me or not. I could be at a party for an hour, get back home to my kid, and spend the rest of the night or following morning blogging about what I'd just witnessed—a perfect solution to my inability to be physically present consistently.

I was zooming from taking classes, working at the bank,

and picking my daughter up from my grandmother Bert, who ran a day care out of her house. On mornings after parties, when I worked my bank teller job, people I saw at warehouse functions the previous night would shuffle up to the counter, not recognizing who I was, though I'd been right next to Abdu while they conversed with him. I was incognito. Sometimes, while running their information to initiate a deposit, I'd notice accounts with balances above $20,000—kids in their early twenties presumably set up to succeed by their moneyed, white families. The same people who would bum pizza and perform financial hardship. The insight helped quell my impostor syndrome, emphasizing that I was from a different universe, and, if anything, my edge was that I could not be attached to one sect of society but, rather, was navigating many in the pursuit to elevate myself.

It started to finally make sense that the whole point of challenging myself creatively wasn't to do so in an isolating, masochistic manner. Sure, I had a kid to feed while everybody else enjoyed more fluidity to their daily happenings, but I had to arrive at a place where I recognized that wasn't a strike against me. It was an advantage. I was, by demands of my responsibilities, required to be disciplined; my creative pursuits had to have real earning potential for them to stick because I wasn't in the position to just do shit for the love. Using time effectively and purposefully is a natural instinct when your time is dictated by a kid's schedule.

Wanting to have more of an impact, along with Abdu, I started looking around the scene, imagining what other possibilities could emerge. We took notes from the best things we observed in the DIY scene: venues with little-to-no rental fee, small runs of themed self-published magazines, relying on the collective resources of friends. We had our own community to lean on— the clusters of people we knew from going to schools all around the city and rubbing shoulders with people in different neighborhoods. "Fuck these other people's parties. They in our city," we'd say to each other. Motivated to act on this newfound pride, we outlined a monthly party series called Guttahball (a literary play on joining authentic inner-city flavor with the communal aspects of queer ballroom culture). The plan was to showcase Baltimore's homegrown Black musical talent and join it with the DIY art-kid scene, as well as to bring in nationally known underground acts who fit into our agenda. We both promoted to our Facebook friends and people we knew personally. Abdu would write the show announcement and find someone to design the flyer. I took the pictures on an old digital camera my uncle gave me and uploaded them to make sure we had documentation. We both put up a couple hundred dollars to pay for any artist we brought from out of town, who would crash on one of our couches.

The party launched at the now-defunct Broom Factory Factory (the BFF) in the spring of 2013. The space was an unsuspecting warehouse down a steep hill in Baltimore's industrial, centrally located Remington neighborhood; rumor was that they had actually made brooms there at some point. But when we caught wind of the place, it was occupied by artists who needed cheap spaces to live while making music or various other forms of art. There was raggedy furniture in every room that appeared to have been retrieved off the street. A kitchen that looked like it belonged to a school cafeteria, and a little patch of a room where they let parties happen—no stage, just a slab of wood on the dirty carpet to designate where performers belonged. Our first big draw was Cities Aviv, a Memphis-raised artist who took pages out of the book of his hometown heroes Three 6 Mafia by pulverizing soul samples down to maddening, yet luxurious loops that played in the background while he wailed into the mic like a punk artist when he wasn't offering gentle melodies. He'd just released a mixtape called *Black Pleasure* through the streetwear brand Mishka—a common practice in the late-stage blog era—and was looking to spread the gospel of his artistry. After his performance, Abdu took the stage and hummed sultry incantations over thumping club music 808s. The late OG Dutch Master—an East Baltimore rapper who helped usher in a local variant of the A$AP Rocky–influenced artful street music for the new generation—offered a set as well. It was the perfect storm of everything we wanted the underground scene to embody with us behind the steering wheel: Black, punk, street, queer, genre defying, disruptive. In the following months we held more iterations of Guttahball with the same mission, each time with more people showing up who craved an environment like the one we were fostering. Photos of a cramped space filled, primarily, with young Black faces began circulating on Facebook and Tumblr. We got included in *City Paper* roundups, and word spread within our peer group about the party's success. To me, we had arrived.

My non-scene life started to work in tandem, as well, with what I had going on creatively; with our party's hyperconcentrated relevance, my outsiderness subsided. I got an apartment on the edge of Charles Village with Abdu and our homey Dennis. I was still working my teller job, but also picked up a handful of hours ushering at the local art-house theater to cement my Different Nigga image. Caring for my daughter became easier as she matured out of toddler age and into her preschool era. The BFF's glory lasted all but six months; naturally, with our party gaining popularity, more young Black people craving a different nightlife experience began booking the space. But in the mostly white, newly gentrified area where the venue stood, people began to complain and call the police to shut down parties. The people living in the space were given an ultimatum: stop throwing shows, or the place would permanently be shut down. Expectedly, they chose shelter.

The next iteration of me and Abdu's stake in the scene came in late 2013 when the Crown, a cramped two-story venue with Korean food, was just getting underway. That's where our KAHLON party was born. It wouldn't be hyperbole to say the Crown changed the trajectory of my life. The same night we launched KAHLON, I debuted my zine, which documented the scene in interviews, album reviews, photo essays, and artist diaries. To ensure the outside world was aware of, and interested in, what Baltimore had going on, I wore the hats of a journalist, a party host, and an all-around advocate. Without that level of participation, I'm not sure what kind of life I would have today. The Crown provided a home base for me to contextualize the ever-evolving nature of Baltimore's musical landscape.

Playing an integral role in helping to materialize an albeit small, but formidable ecosystem in my hometown did wonders for my self-confidence and creative progression. I mattered in this space, my friends mattered in this space, and our dedication to creating a much-needed outlet mattered enough to people outside this space that they wanted to take part in it. And with

Abdu, I fortified a real artistic partnership. Between booking artists from other places to come to Baltimore, and him traveling to do DIY shows in different parts of the country, our networks expanded. We could go to NYC, Philly, DC, or as far as Austin and have someone to connect with for a place to stay or new people we should meet. Compared to the agonizing hours I was logging at my various other jobs, I felt purpose and optimism here.

In the summer of 2024, the Crown announced it was permanently closing, shutting the doors on an era pivotal to my development. What I'll miss most about that time is the exhilaration of early adulthood, of world building; the assurance that your vision and ideals are reflected in a community. Young creatives, more than anything, need to be told yes to their ideas, not inundated with hindsight-driven advice. The Crown told me and Abdu yes when we wanted to make it KAHLON's permanent home. And the Crown told others with lofty ideas yes when they didn't feel quite at home anywhere else. For all those green lights, I'm thankful. But the Crown's power isn't necessarily in the physical place. It's in the experiences, the opportunities to grow and evolve, the ability to relay stories from those times to serve as inspiration to new generations as they carve out their own spaces.

During this time in my life, when I had to constantly fight tooth and nail against limitations in my mind of what was possible for me, it was absolutely crucial that I established a friendship with Abdu. Being invited into his world, I learned countless valuable lessons from the Black queer community, who have the admirable gift of—often as a means of survival—creating worlds for themselves where the restrictions of the normie realm don't exist, even if just for abbreviated moments. I owe so much of my ability, at that time, to block out the pressures to conform to those artists. They showed me how to dream. And how to storm forward even when things aren't exactly how you want them to be, for the promise of them becoming what you need them to be if you stay the course.

GOOD GOVERNMENT JOB

B EING BLIND IN ONE eye has only benefited me twice in life. The first time was in the fall of 2009 when, nearly two years after the car accident that altered my sight, I won close to $60,000 in a case against the other driver's insurance company. I'd just turned nineteen and had returned to Baltimore after a year of college in Brooklyn. At that stage of my life, I probably never had more than $500 in my possession at one time. I felt rich. When the money finally cleared in my account, I walked into a CarMax and bought a 2006 smoke-gray Nissan Altima in full for $12,000, the first whip I ever owned. Bear's Den, a tattoo shop on Route 40, saw me twice within a few week's time: the obligatory roaring lion on my left shoulder and a Black Power first with sun rays coming out of it on the right side of my chest. Every pair of Nike Foamposites that I couldn't afford before was purchased for criminally high resale prices: the eggplants, coppers, silver joints from back in the day with the black check, the pearls, and the university blues. I drove four hours up to SoHo to Pharrell's BBC store and copped $500 jackets. Home-cooked meals fell completely out of my diet. My palate craved what I perceived to be the finer things in life— Jack Daniel's chicken-and-shrimp from TGI Fridays, pasta from the Cheesecake Factory, and bushels of jumbo male crabs. And

I was too good to go to the movie theaters I'd attended when I was broke; instead, I took the hour drive down to DC to see films at the AMC in Georgetown. Before the settlement, I was working as a part-time sales associate at DSW, but aimlessly walking around and harassing people to sign up for memberships while they tried on shoes when I had tens of thousands of dollars in my bank account started to feel beneath me, so I quit. Within a year's time of riding high, I blew every cent.

The second time being blind in one eye benefited me was in 2014. I was tired of seesawing between having apartments and moving back in with my mother because my rent couldn't consistently be paid with part-time jobs and irregular freelance writing assignments. My aunt Joanie worked at the Social Security Administration, which offered some of the most coveted jobs for people in the Baltimore area for their stability, potential for long-term employment, and generous benefits package. Down on my luck, I leaned on everybody in my family who worked in an office for leads on openings. After months of not getting any calls back, Joanie called me with an urgent tip: "They don't do this very often, but right now, SSA has some openings in my office for people with disabilities. It's called the Schedule A program, and they have to meet a quota every eighteen months or so. All you gotta do is have your doctor confirm that you're legally blind in that eye and I'll see what I can do." *This might be my chance to actually get my shit together and become a productive adult,* I thought. My ego had taken a number of hits by this time. My daughter was almost four years old, and I still wasn't in a place where I could fully uphold my end of the bargain, having to lean on family for resources. My writing career wasn't much of one to speak of, considering no one would hire me to do it full-time, and didn't even contribute regularly enough to make a financial impact. Change was paramount.

After two months of calling the SSA office on Woodlawn Drive and waiting around due to budgetary restrictions for new hires, I finally got an email back:

Mr. Burney,

Good News! A meeting was held to discuss our budget situation and we are now able to interview for this position. Please accept our apology for the prior decision to not interview and any inconveniences that it may have caused. Thank you, again, for your interest in the position of Earnings Specialist with the Social Security Administration. We have scheduled an interview for you.

Within a few weeks I was hired and signed a contract to make $30,761 annually, before taxes. I didn't care how low or high the salary would be, I just knew I finally had the first real job of my life, one that gave me health insurance, a cubicle, and a significant amount of overtime. Earnings Specialist was a roundabout way of saying my role was to sit at an ancient computer and figure out if the amount of income companies were digitally filing into the system matched what they actually made. The more discrepancies solved, the better. It wasn't complicated work; no jobs in these sorts of environments are. They're just simple enough to allow you to remain perpetually on autopilot, accepting your position as an insignificant cog in the system.

Shortly after getting acclimated to the flow of things, I learned that everyone who sat in my immediate vicinity not only did a variation of the same job but, like me, got to SSA through the Schedule A program. While my disability wasn't detectable without me volunteering the information to someone, my coworkers endured a deep variety of conditions. Cory, a middle-aged brother from DC and the occupant of my next-door cubicle, had a severe case of narcolepsy and would start snoring literally seconds after having a conversation with you. Sarah Lee, an older white woman from Highlandtown, didn't have any discernible ailments outside being close to six hundred pounds and not able to walk for more than a few steps before needing to gather herself. Anthony, a brother from Northwood with the best sense of humor on our floor and an impeccable collection of Ralph Lauren polos, had one leg that was shorter than the other, so he walked with a sort of gallop. All the others were older Black women who'd been working at the agency for well over thirty years and would, upon arrival at the office, turn their chairs out to face the others in the aisle and gossip for most of the day about people on other floors of the building. Government jobs are predicated on a grade system—a hierarchy that everyone is incentivized to be hyperaware of at all times—the highest being a GS-15, meaning you're making six figures and can tell niggas what to do. Daily, when someone was talking behind another person's back, they'd refer to them by grade as a sign of contempt or condescension: "Oh, so-and-so? She a Grade Twelve, that's why she walking around here like she better than everybody." I—a trainee-level GS-4—had no interest in excelling, so from early on, I fished for ways to cheat the system while pursuing my actual passion.

By 2014, I'd been contributing to a number of respected cultural publications for a little over a year. The *Baltimore City Paper*, a now-shuttered alt weekly, was my most consistent landing spot. For them, I'd cover what was happening in the city's underground, writing articles about rappers making a name for themselves on the scene, the best parties to attend, and the occasional film review. I'd go to the parties and interview Mighty Mark, TT the Artist, Butch Dawson, and Abdu about the new emerging youth culture. It was the work I wanted to spend my every waking moment doing. The paper rarely denied my ideas, but never paid me more than $150, making my contributions feel more like a side hustle to buy weed and offset the cost of a small monthly bill. I was starting to land some reviews on *Pitchfork* for artists from different pockets of the country who belonged to a similar alternative ecosystem: B L A C K I E, the new crop of DC rappers replacing go-go music as the most sought after genre among the youth, and the work of Mykki Blanco, a rapper who was kicking down the door for a wave of queer artists with newfound visibility. The same month I started at SSA, VICE's music section, *Noisey*, accepted a pitch of mine to ride down to Virginia Beach to hang out with an artist I found out about online named DRAM. He sang like a lost member of Parliament-Funkadelic, but on contemporary rap beats. So one weekend, I hit 95 South with my homeboys Keem and Greedy in the '06 Altima—now a shell of itself compared to when I bought it with car-accident money five years earlier—to conduct an interview about how his breakout single "Cha Cha" was starting to make its rounds locally. I traveled on my own dime, to prove I was dedicated to getting stories by any means and to potentially convince editors that I might be someone they'd want to bring on for more consistent assignments.

As big of a deal it was for me to land these gigs, the opportunities were too sparse to make a real dent. But I was determined to make it shake. Barely a month into my new job, I was already spending more time at my desk sneaking to write and send pitches out than investigating if a hardware store in Frankfort, Kentucky, or a chiropractor's office in Lewiston, Maine, was accurately filing their taxes. The big boss pulled me aside in late November: "Lawrence, I've been made aware that you are only resolving three cases per day, when the average should be somewhere in the thirties. We can see in the system you're spending time doing other things on the computer. Please be advised that you are on probationary status."

Time moves depressingly slowly in a cubicle environment when you hate what you're doing day-to-day. I kept relatively sane by watching the entirety of *The Wire* for the first time on my phone within two weeks, essentially letting episodes run without pausing. Whenever a new album dropped, I had the privilege of dissecting it with my undivided attention, which served well for my development as a writer. The day Kendrick Lamar dropped *To Pimp a Butterfly*, I ran the album back three straight times, luxuriating in what felt like a pivotal moment in my generation, completely uninterrupted outside the occasional snore from Cory.

For my mental well-being—or its detriment—I accepted that I'd be working at SSA for the foreseeable future and continued on the path of doing the bare minimum while fitting in time to pursue my writerly aspirations. Within a year of starting, I moved out of my mother's house for good and found a two-bedroom apartment in Reservoir Hill for $900—the first time I was able to provide my daughter with her own room. After rent, utilities, car insurance, and other expenses, the $30,000 annual salary was just enough for me to not starve, so I had to start working overtime—a couple extra hours after my regular shift or the beginning of my Saturdays from 8:00 a.m. to 1:00 p.m.—to give myself more of a cushion. I was now seeing Cory, Sarah Lee, Anthony, and Miss Ilene more than my own family and friends, having to endure their annoying, albeit hilarious, eccentricities regularly. Sarah Lee, when taking breaks from her work, spent her time loudly professing how she lived vicariously through demonstrative Black women on TV. "Ugh, I wish I was Cookie Lyon," she sighed one day, talking about Taraji P. Henson's character on *Empire*. "She's a fucking boss." While we worked on a Saturday, after I told Sarah Lee and Miss Ilene—a grandmotherly Black woman who sat behind me—about the Mars One mission to send people to outer space, Miss Ilene replied, "I bet it ain't no Black people doing that crazy mess."

Sarah Lee looked up the participants and debunked Miss Ilene's assumption, pointing out a Black scientist who'd signed up.

"Let me see," Miss Ilene said, walking up to the computer screen. "She's African. Like I said, ain't none of *us* doing that."

Meanwhile, Cory was going through a turbulent stint with his wife, whom he caught cheating. "If I don't walk away, I'm gonna end up killing this woman," I overheard him tearfully telling his father on the phone through the thin fabric cubicle wall that separated us.

I was being sucked into this painfully pedestrian lifestyle and needed to find a way out.

In Maryland, or any of the land relatively close to Washington, DC, government jobs are the crown jewel of the employment market. Having one gives you an air of prestige, especially in the Black community. You're more stable than the average person you know; you've got that regular paycheck and the good benefits. Your pension is rock-solid. It's also incredibly hard to lose an agency job once you've reached permanent status. Systems are put in place so that instead of firing someone, they are offered counseling if they're falling off their square. People will throw out "I work for the federal government" like they have the security clearance to walk through the White House and have lunch with Obama on a casual Thursday, when all they do is work a glorified paper-filing job. It's not typically a place that you ever leave. And they set up offices in a way so that you'd—by conventional standards—be insane to even consider going elsewhere. The first floor of our office housed a convenience store where you could get your favorite snacks and play the lottery, so you wouldn't have to leave the premises. There was a bank inside, where, if you had an account, you'd be paid a day or two earlier than everyone else. People developed long-standing friendships that helped them get through the time served in the work setting.

The security made me sick to my stomach. No self-respecting twenty-four-year-old should have that much stability at their disposal. I felt I was gradually falling into a puddle of quicksand and, every day, I was inching closer to drowning. Not to mention, my writing didn't seem like it was getting me any closer to an escape. I was still landing pieces with *City Paper* and VICE, but my contributions to places like *Complex*, *Pitchfork*, and *XXL* were too sparse to make a difference. My favorite magazine was *The*

FADER, as they aligned more closely to my worldview than any other publication. Instead of relegating emerging artists to brief lists, they gave ample space to people who operated on the margins, fully contextualizing what made their music special with multiple-page spreads and beautiful photography. The writers I most admired—smart, culturally in the know, with impeccable taste, unforgivingly critical when need be—such as Rawiya Kameir, Jason Parham, and Doreen St. Félix, had their work featured there regularly. But for whatever reason, whenever I sent *The FADER* pitches from my SSA cubicle, I'd get rejected. It was a major hit to my confidence. *Maybe I'm not as good as I think I am,* I'd think, stuck browsing through tax filings. A future in which writing was nothing more than a side hustle from my government job felt like the most realistic possibility for me.

One day in the office, Anthony walked over to my desk with a card that needed to be signed. It was a congratulatory gesture for Miss Barbara, whom I'd only spoken to in passing when I walked by her cubicle. The plan was to surprise her with a cake and gifts. The occasion? "She been working here for sixty fucking years, dawg," Anthony told me, shaking his head. "She retired seven years ago, got bored, and came back to start working again." I signed my name, and after lunch that da, we gathered around to celebrate Miss Barbara's sixth decade of service. While everyone stood around her and honored the milestone, she sat and looked around. She couldn't stand on her own anymore and didn't feel like depending on her walker. In her eighties, she'd given all of her life to this job, working here since she was the same age as me. She'd probably watched her colleagues grow from young adults to great-grandparents, listened to the radio newscast of Martin

Luther King being shot in Memphis, had coworkers leave this earthly plane, all while being at this same place. It launched me into an existential crisis, staring off into space thinking about how I'd rather die at this very instant than to give these niggas all the good years of my life for some shit that didn't fulfill me. It wasn't any shade toward Miss Barbara; sixty years ago, this was probably one of the most prestigious occupations a Black person could have around these parts. I just couldn't fathom the idea of the same thing happening for me.

After the celebration, I went back to my desk and let out a deep sigh before signing back into the ancient computer with its black screen and green type, flipping through tax filings that were starting to look identical to me. On the regular PC monitor, I logged in to my Gmail account and noticed a message from an editor at *The FADER* who'd turned down the last three pitches I'd sent over. Maybe I'd sent over an idea that I forgot about, and they were going to tell me this one wouldn't work either. Instead, it read, "Hey Lawrence! Hope all is well. Yo Gotti is coming to NYC next weekend to perform and we're curious to know if you'd be open to coming up to spend time with him for an interview that'll run on the site." I put my head down and wept uncontrollably—tears of relief, but also of frustration and hope. A needed sign that my current position wasn't permanent, but rather a period I needed to get through to get to the other side.

MR. MOONEY &
THE COMPLEXION
FOR THE
PROTECTION

I F YOU ARE OLD enough to remember watching *Seinfeld*, then you are old enough to remember when Michael Richards, the man who plays the show's zany jester Kramer, went off the rails during a stand-up performance at LA's Laugh Factory in 2006 and repeatedly hurled the word *nigger* at a Black man in the crowd for allegedly heckling him. The footage of the incident, even twenty years later, is a lot to take in. Comedians deal with being interrupted in a variety of ways. Some use it as an opportunity to work the detracting party into the routine they already planned on executing. Some find a way to convince the person in the crowd to chill or threaten to throw them out of the show. But Richards was so incensed at the man for talking during his set he had to exercise, what he thought, was the most effective way to reclaim power over the space: by reminding a nigger of their rightful place within society.

Richards set the tone of his explosion up so people could fully understand what he meant. "Fifty years ago, we'd have you upside down with a fucking fork up your ass," he yells to the man. Feels appropriate to assume Richards was referring to the public lynching of Black people that was once prevalent in places where niggers lived in significant numbers, often spearheaded by white people like Richards who resented how freely Black people were able to move (which wasn't even all that free). Footage of the incident doesn't reveal how the exchange got so heated, but the first time Richards let the word fly, the crowd was still chuckling from the beginning of the argument. But by the time he blurted it out again, the room had gone uncomfortably silent, except for a lone woman's voice exhaling, "Oh my God," in disbelief. Enraged, Richards kept going until a back-and-forth ensued with another Black person in the crowd who reminded him that, outside of his portrayal of Kramer, he was a nobody and maybe this episode was an explanation as to why he hadn't landed any more prominent roles on-screen.

When the situation made its rounds in the media, things obviously did not go over well with the Black community, or with most non-Blacks who appeared to be liberal in their politics. It was on every major news station and late-night television talk show and discussed at dinner tables throughout the country. "Man done lost his mind" and things of that nature are what I remember hearing. Jesse Jackson called for a nationwide ban of the word, from all races, to finally do away with something that'd been harming folks for far too long.

One of the biggest supporters of this initiative, surprisingly, was the comedian Paul Mooney, whose career had largely revolved around commenting on racial dynamics within American society—and who absolutely adored the word *nigga*. Mooney went on a mini-press-run of sorts, saying he had had "a romance with the word," but something about hearing it used with such vitriol in public, six years after the dawn of a new millennium, gave him an out-of-body experience, one in which he recognized the word's toxicity and its inability of being separated from its violent origins. Similar to how a smoker can overlook the hygienic and health-related consequences of their habit until they enter another smoker's space and are forced to reflect on how they show up in the world. To Mooney, it was a realization that the word hadn't actually been fully reclaimed, and that a person could still lean on it to cause harm. Maybe he was shocked at his ability to still be hurt by something he thought he'd already conquered.

Mooney was born in Shreveport, Louisiana, to teenage parents in August of 1941, before relocating as a child to Oakland, where he was primarily raised by his grandmother. Life split between the Deep South and the Bay Area—a breeding ground of Black radical thought—informed Mooney's matter-of-fact stance on how race works in America and who bears the brunt of its consequences. After a short stint in the military, where instead of being sent off to battle, he was assigned to an entertainment troupe after wowing his fellow servicemen at a talent show, he returned to California and helped establish an all-Black improv group called the Yankee Doodle Bedbugs. Then he headed down to Hollywood to ingratiate himself with the players. That's where he met Richard Pryor, who became a dear friend and a collaborator; their artistic connection would result in long, fruitful careers for both. Both Pryor and Mooney performed in the style of their predecessors Redd Foxx and Dick Gregory, who leaned into the paradoxes of living in a Jim Crow society. Where Black people couldn't express their disdain and disapproval of living in a country dominated by racist white people, Foxx and Gregory took on the role of being a voice for the subdued; the cushion of comedy provided them the opportunity.

As society got incrementally more liberal for race relations, Mooney, as Pryor's writer and a solo performer, made sure to leave ample space to speak to the fallacy of perceived white superiority. "My white friends, I had to get rid of them," Mooney said to a small crowd during a performance in 1973, speaking to the inequality baked into American life. "Because we went into a whole new era then I became a negro. Now that is difficult. When you have to be a negro, it is rough. I had my briefcase and my white voice trying to get jobs and trying to be educated. I used to go home so tired. Another day of being a negro, I can't take it!" He continued a legacy of Black comics who allowed people to laugh at something that was truly ridiculous, as we all know it to be. The following decades of his career, working with Pryor, Redd Foxx, and, later, Dave Chappelle, Mooney explored the ways race and the word *nigga*—both literally and figuratively—ruled our every move in this country.

Mooney granted Fox News an interview two days after the incident at the Laugh Factory; he said after seeing the footage, he felt like he was inside a Klan rally. When journalist Greta Van Susteren asked what Richards could do to redeem himself, Mooney said, "He can take that same act and perform it at the Apollo, then he can come talk to me. Or he can host the BET Hip-Hop Awards." If not anger, there was palpable annoyance in his voice. But then, a week later, in an interview with NPR, Mooney presented a different stance. After some reflection and a conversation with Richards, he took it easy on Mr. Kramer, citing the incident as a legitimate (albeit racist) nervous breakdown, one so far from whom he'd known Richards to be in their previous interactions. Mooney used the NPR interview as an opportunity for introspection, admitting that he had had a love for the word and couldn't see a future in which he wouldn't use it, but thanks to Richards, he now saw that it was a weapon and nothing more. "It was like a nuclear bomb, and it just hit me. He was actually my Dr. Phil—he cured me with the word." To put into context how crazy it was for Mooney to disavow *nigga*, it's like if Steph Curry took a pledge to stop shooting 3s, Charles Barkley removed *turrble* from his lexicon, or Shaun King stopped making GoFundMes.

The ironic thing about this proclamation is that, in the following year, Mooney released a stand-up special called *Know Your History: Jesus Is Black; So Was Cleopatra*. For over an hour, he based his thesis around the ridiculousness of how race is performed, interpreted, and policed in our everyday lives, often to a point that drives us to collective mania. The special was released on DVD in February of 2007, but it must have been filmed before Michael Richards's racist tirade in November of 2006 because, throughout, not only does Mooney say *nigga* repeatedly—as he always did—but he challenges people who take issue with the word being uttered at all. "I've been a nigga for a very long time. When it was important, nobody said nothing. Now it don't mean shit, everybody got something to say about it," he offered. "I have been called it enough, I'll say it any fucking time I feel like it. I say it one hundred times every morning when I wake up. It makes my teeth white. Nigga, nigga, nigga, nigga, nigga . . . " This is the romance he spoke of in that 2006 interview with NPR—of a marriage to something you know so intimately, you have a hard time letting it go even when it doesn't serve you.

The first time I watched that special was in the living room of my grandparents' house, sometime during my junior year in high school. I'd known Mooney through his appearances in the "Negrodamus" and "Ask a Black Dude" sketches on *Chappelle's Show*, both of which I loved for their candor. But in watching this special with my grandparents, I was given a crash course on his résumé as Black comedy's most lethal secret weapon for what had been three decades at that point. Stand-up and comedic sitcoms were big in our household, as they were in many Black families of the time. My family preferred a rawness to their comedy, the type where Black people spoke to Black people about Black issues, even if others wanted to participate as onlookers. Whether it was Redd Foxx, Bernie Mac, Bruce Bruce, Mo'Nique, our household comedy made light of the Black struggle and pointed a sharp tongue toward white supremacist structures. In the living room that day, my family pointed out how Mooney had written some of Richard Pryor's best material, including the infamous 1975 "Word Association" skit on *SNL* where Pryor and comedian Chevy Chase stage a contentious job interview in which the two trade insults; the last of which is Chase calling Pryor a "nigger" with considerable force in the -*er*. Mooney was also tasked with choosing the talent for Pryor's short-lived, self-titled NBC series, which included rising superstars within the art form like Robin Williams, John Witherspoon, Sandra Bernhard, and Tim Reid. My family told me Mooney created *In Living Color*'s Homey D. Clown character, whose antics (terrorizing schoolchildren with below-the-belt insults) brought me immense pleasure as a young child.

And my family mentioned how, in the eighties, Mooney had been part of an Eddie Murphy–led collective of comic elites called the Black Pack, which included Robert Townsend, Arsenio Hall, and Keenen Ivory Wayans. *Know Your History* was framed as a sort of retrospective for Mooney's career. By the time the special came out, a lot of people, like me, were unaware of his contribution to comedic history. As Pryor's career trailed off in the latter years of his life, so did Mooney's opportunities in Hollywood. Being on *Chappelle's Show* introduced him to a new generation that, otherwise, might not have understood his impact. Throughout the special, Mooney suggests his career was ultimately stifled by his commitment to discussing the racial schism that informs American life. In those eighty-three minutes, he masterfully articulates the conspiratorial inclinations that Black Americans live with, a sort of nod to acknowledge that we're not crazy for thinking some foul play is going on. And he leans on pop culture to lay out the many ways: HBO using *Oz* to frame Black men in prison as savage, while *The Sopranos* humanized Italian mobsters who took part in the same brutal behavior; the tight-lipped, anger-suppressing smirks from white Hollywood elites as Three 6 Mafia's "It's Hard Out Here for a Pimp" took the Oscar for Best Original Song in 2006; the irony of Mickey Mouse's minstrel roots while the Mickey Mouse Club rarely had Black Mouseketeers. Yes, racism can be overt in this country, but generally speaking, it's a little more insidious in how it operates. Life often feels like the white power structures are saying to us, *We're gonna place you in this position, but we're gonna obscure why you're in that position. And we're gonna conceal how we block you out of opportunities for advancement, but frame it in*

*a way that makes you feel like there's something intrinsically wrong
with you.*

In the special, Mooney pokes at how other non-Black races in
America buy into this propaganda until they get what he calls
the Nigga Wake-Up Call. One of the first instances he uses as an
example is the Mexican community in Los Angeles, who, at the
time, were facing an incredible threat of mass deportation. It's
uncomfortable, at times, seeing him celebrate forceable removal,
but I don't think that's what Mooney is really trying to express here.
He's underlining how, under this system, nobody is secure, and no
matter how much people within, say, the Mexican or Korean or
whatever community think they have a closer proximity to whiteness, and thus hierarchy over Black people, there will always be
a time when whiteness reminds us who is and isn't worthy of the
ruling class distinction. In his own way, I believe Mooney was trying to emphasize that a certain kind of class solidarity was necessary for all of us to rise up out of this predicament. That's what
I hear when he says Samoans are nothing but Some More Niggas
or that the indigenous people of the Philippines were Black—not
to strip away what qualities make those folks distinctive, but to
emphasize that everyone gets their chance being the nigger. For
just as long as the nigger has been a person of African descent, it
could very well be a Southeast Asian, Muslim American, or Eastern European.

I sat watching *Know Your History* in awe, mainly because it'd
been the first time I'd seen a stand-up who affirmed the way I
learned about race in my household and in my community. My
immediate family's outlook on life as Black people aligned with
Paul Mooney's. They were weary of white people, hypervigilant

when dealing with folks outside the Black American community out of concern for their potential superiority complex, and they knew the fix was in place for us to be railroaded at every turn. To see an artist stand firm in these values was freeing. It affirmed a oneness experienced throughout each corner of Black America that, when you're still coming up, you aren't fully aware of. I was affirmed.

The sentiments he expressed in the stand-up made his call to do away with a racial slur that we'd already reclaimed (or so I thought) all the more shocking. In those waves of interviews Mooney did in response to Michael Richards, his concern was that, even though *nigga/er* was starting to be used by non-Black people with heightened frequency, it was added insult that those people didn't actually stand in community with us, beyond extraction.

In high school, right before I saw *Know Your History*, I became fairly cordial with a white boy named Jeff. He was drawn to me and my friends, volunteering himself to partner up with us whenever the class assignment required group work. From what I remember, he grew up somewhere around Dundalk, a poor, working-class white-majority neighborhood on the outskirts of Southeast Baltimore that is often the subject of jokes about rednecks, sewage-like smells, and weird accents. In terms of class, most white people from that side of town ain't doing much better than Black folks, if at all. But they're still white and still carry an air of feeling like that means something significant. One day, presumably feeling enticed by our colloquial flavor at the classroom table, Jeff asked, "Can I say it?" I looked at him, genuinely confused. "Say what?"

"You know, can I say the N-word? Just one time. Please." Me and my two buddies at the table—both Black—looked at one another, then looked back at Jeff and said to do whatever he wanted to do, just be prepared to get knocked the fuck out if he ever tried to pull that in front of us. He was too thirsty, too giddy to align himself with an experience that he didn't have and never would no matter how hard he tried. Even if he grew up piss-poor in Dundalk, it was evident he was daydreaming about what it'd look like for him if he knew Black people cosigned his use of a word that he clearly already used behind closed doors. It would mean that he *is* a nigga. It'd be a stretch to say I was surprised; I'd been warned by my family to be cautious of white people's antics on matters of race. I was taken aback by his nerve to think I was a person who might let him slide.

Years after we graduated, I browsed through my Facebook feed and stumbled on Jeff's page. His look had transitioned from goofy, baby-faced boy with stringy golden-blond hair to the textbook getup of blue-collar white dude who likes nonwhite women: a short haircut that connects to a sharp chin-strap beard, black-ink tattoos on his arms. Under a photo he posted, another Dundalk-looking white guy affectionately commented, "Bro Bro." Jeff responded, "Already my nigga." As a grown man, he'd decided that he didn't need permission anymore. He was gonna be a nigga no matter what anybody else felt.

When, on his song "Euphoria," Kendrick Lamar said he didn't like when Drake said "nigga" during the two's epic, all-out rap battle, Kendrick wasn't really trying to question Aubrey Graham's genetic makeup. For all intents and purposes, Drake is a Black man in the Western sensibility. His being raised by his white Jewish mother in a favorable Toronto neighborhood doesn't negate that. Neither does his role playing a corny teenager on the 2000s-era Canadian TV series *Degrassi*. What Kendrick was pointing toward is how his adversary chooses to show up culturally, and when. Hip-hop rose out of an intense class struggle in the South Bronx and eventually spread to other parts of the country among youth who related to experiencing that disparity and needed a way to articulate the frustration of feeling like there were limited routes to escape these desperate predicaments. The typical touch points of this struggle are police violence, bouts with addiction, and an innate desire to want to liberate yourself to help your family, who spends every day under those conditions.

Even as rap has catapulted itself to the most influential form of music in present-day popular culture, there are conventions within the music that stay true on varying levels. Being anti-establishment (regardless of the establishment) is one of them; as is standing with people who are, in one way or another, trying to raise awareness of issues that are particular to the Black community at any given time. Drake doesn't do too much of that. Throughout his career, he's made it abundantly clear that being a ubiquitous popstar is his top priority, and if he gets around to it, he might put out a contrived statement in support for someone who's been wronged by the system. None of his music goes into detail about how these systems hold people down; no commentary about how that oppression occurs on a global scale or even in his hometown of Toronto. (Imagine how, if moved to do so, he could present the world with virtually untapped knowledge of politics and racial dynamics in Canada.) When videos of young Black American men being murdered by cops and vigilantes were being uploaded to the internet, Kendrick Lamar dedicated an album to the struggle. Meanwhile, Drake made more songs for the club. The reason Kendrick wants to strip away Drake's Black card so badly is because Drake appears as someone who only comes around during the good times. He wants to pop bottles with niggas, go to strip clubs with niggas, and inspire dance moves with niggas. But when it's time to use his outlandishly large platform to truly advocate for niggas, he's nowhere to be found.

Paul Mooney was presented the opportunity to leave the word *nigga* in the rearview two decades before Kramer lost his shit. It happened when, in 1982, Richard Pryor returned from Kenya, where his concept of race, from a Westernized point of view, was permanently altered. According to Pryor, a voice came to him and asked him to look around to see if he noticed any niggas. To that, he answered, there weren't any, even though he was in a country that was almost exclusively Black. The realization drove the comedian to tears after he sat with the fact that he hadn't said or even thought the word for the entire three weeks he was there. At home, he recognized the Black people as niggas because that's what his brain had been programmed to think whenever he laid his eyes on his own community, even when he thought he was subverting the word from its original intent. Because of this, Pryor vowed to never call another Black person nigga ever again.

Mooney confessed in the 2006 NPR interview that he had his own suspicions about the decision because, coincidently, his long-time friend's career became significantly more sustainable and fruitful after pledging to leave *nigga* in the past. Conspiracy or not, it was true; a year after having a *nigga*-less vocabulary, Pryor signed a five-year, $40 million contract with Columbia Pictures and played in *Superman III*. He even briefly hosted a knockoff *Sesame Street* kind of show called *Pryor's Place* in 1984. As sincere as his stance may have been, some Hollywood suits found the decision to be something worth rewarding. It's funny how that works; the same folks whose forefathers branded Pryor with the distinction were uncomfortable with him and Mooney reminding them of the fact, so much so that they made sure to propel him over his peers for "evolving" beyond the need to do so. Reluctantly, Mooney helped Pryor write the bits in which he shared with his audience this epiphany to cleanse himself during the *Live on the Sunset Strip Tour* in '82, but Mooney personally wasn't going to retire from using the word anytime soon. "We had made money off the word, we had got famous off the word. And we were married to it," he reflected. "I said, 'Richard, how could you give that up?' It was such a tool. But I was wrong and he was totally right," Mooney said to NPR.

Michael Richards effectively vanished for nearly twenty years after his outburst at the Laugh Factory—too ashamed to face the public. But in 2024, he resurfaced with a memoir titled *Entrances and Exits*, which presumably touches on that disgraced night, among other things. While on a press run for the book, he sat down with *Today's* Hoda Kotb, who, before anything else, asked him in what ways, eighteen years later, was he different from the man we last saw having that racist rant. To that, Richards answered, "Probably more aware of myself. Anger, looking at it very closely, it's something that's always with me. It had ahold of me. I canceled myself out . . . to see what the heck was going on inside me." If words or expressions mean anything, he appeared remorseful, but it's hard to see a future in which that storied night doesn't define his career, at least to Black people who once enjoyed him on *Seinfeld*. Paul Mooney didn't live to see Richards's attempt at redemption. In 2021, Mooney died of a heart attack at the age of seventy-nine, but not before dedicating his life to the cause of helping Black Americans (or all Americans, for that matter) gain a better understanding of how whiteness works. Because, even after doing the unthinkable, whiteness will allow its worst deeds to be forgiven. At least glossed over. It reminds me of the only time I saw Mooney live.

In June of 2013, he did a weekend of shows at the Baltimore Comedy Factory. I attended with my homeboy Dennis. As with most comedy shows, recording the routine on a phone or taking photos wasn't permitted. During his performance, a white couple was warned by a Black security guard about pulling their phones out to take pictures. Minutes after the guard left, they started recording again. He warned them again, nicely. But within another few minutes, they went right back to their antics. The last time, the security guard got forceful with them and escorted them out. Paul Mooney sat watching in amusement. White couples leaving his shows—usually by choice after being offended— were common. "Don't worry, they'll be back," he said, laughing. "They're gonna go talk to the owner and they'll be back in a few minutes. They're white. They always win." A few more minutes passed, and like clockwork the man of the couple came walking back in. "See! I told you. White people never get in trouble," Mooney pointed out. Turns out, the man left his jacket. And the crowd laughed in unison as he took his final walk of shame.

BRUISED

I N THE FALL OF 2016, I left my cheap, nicely renovated apartment in the Southwest Baltimore ruins to go sleep on a bed-frameless mattress in a room I was subletting from a liberal white couple in the Bushwick section of Brooklyn. The last time I'd lived in New York City, I was an eighteen-year-old college freshman satisfied with the freedom of being away from home, and enjoying the pleasures of arguing with Izzy, Dennis, Glen, and the guys in my dorm about why French Montana could never be a better or more innovative rapper than Gucci Mane. Setting myself up for a prosperous adulthood hardly crossed my mind then. But as a twenty-six-year-old in 2016, the urgency to make something of myself was constant, almost to a level of desperation.

A year earlier, I'd finessed my way into walking the stage at the University of Baltimore's graduation while still owing four classes worth of credits that I never planned on finishing because I needed to fully pursue life in the real world. I had a six-year-old daughter whom I needed to provide for, and the way life was going, my most persistent fear was a future in which I equated my unrealized ambitions with her existence. Just before the move back to Brooklyn, I quit my job at Social Security as an Earnings Specialist, with no real backup plan other than using my Hyundai Sonata to do Uber, selling the magazines I made, and chasing music publications down for freelance assignments. Betting on myself wasn't working the way black-turtleneck-wearing YouTube entrepreneurs say it will, but my spirit was withering under fluorescent office lights and round-the-clock snoring from my next-cubicle neighbor. I had to try something else.

Uber was hell. The only traction came from circling around the places white people congregated on weekend nights in Baltimore, competing against every other driver with the same routine. One early-summer evening after dropping an auntie off around Mondawmin, my Uber account stopped working. Trying to figure it out, I went to my email, where, twenty minutes earlier, I got a message from the company stating my account was on a temporary hold. A customer from the day before filed a complaint: "The driver's car had a strong smell of marijuana." I knew exactly who it was. A lily-white family I'd picked up around Fells Point whose arrival into my car made me realize I had a bag of herb in my glove compartment. My phony tucked-lip smile, half-hearted greeting, hands firmly on the wheel, and Fela Kuti's *Army Arrangement* album playing on medium-low volume wasn't enough of a gesture of respectability to prevent them from pulling a police move behind my back. I replied the only way any self-respecting negro would: "Hello, I'm extremely troubled by this message. I would never ride around with drugs in my car and feel that the customer made assumptions based on my race. I would appreciate it if this hold on my account was lifted." I hit send, unconsciously opened Twitter, and saw that VICE's music publication, *Noisey*, was hiring for a staff writer. I was already a somewhat regular contributor there, and with my cash flow in limbo, I decided to go after it, even though it felt impossible.

From the time my daughter was born, I coparented with her mother, setting her on a course of zigzagging akin to my own upbringing. A couple days each week with me, a couple with her mom, weekends alternating between us, and touching base at both grandmothers' houses on what felt like daily. I'd gone the entirety of my abbreviated adulthood never spending more than a week apart from my daughter. The thought of uprooting myself from that fixed schedule scared the shit out of me, not only because she'd never experienced life another way, but also because I was worried about what or whom she would be experiencing with more distance from me. Outside of my cousin Aaron, Little Al at church, Miles, and my homegirl Ashley, I didn't know anybody who had both of their parents under one roof. And even though mine weren't either, my father took me to all my doctors' appointments, established his presence with faculty members at my schools during my early years, and showed up swiftly when there were emergencies. That was more hands-on activity than mostly anybody else's pops I knew.

I used that track record as a barometer to measure what *real* fatherhood looked like. Anything less, in my paranoid mind, might earn me the label of a deadbeat. But it felt like I'd run out of options in Baltimore. The magazines and newspapers in town, even though they loved covering the pain and eccentricities of Black folks, didn't appear interested in hiring ones from the city. The jobs I did have access to were soul-sucking and fast-track routes to a life devoid of fulfillment. So, I reached out to my daughter's mother and prepared for her to justifiably hit me with disapproval over how my coparenting from two hundred miles away wasn't feasible, let alone fair to her. "I just feel like, in the long run, I'll be able to do way more for her if I take this chance. It would set me up for a better future," I said over the phone while sitting in my Sonata. "If I get it, I'll be down here every week if need be. It can be figured out." To my surprise, she was accepting of the move. I could breathe easier knowing that one of the main hurdles had been cleared. A few weeks later, VICE called me up to Brooklyn for an interview, and a couple weeks after that, they offered me the job.

In transitioning, I felt encouraged by the exchange I had with my daughter's mother and wanted to continue with what felt like a new chapter of mature, grown-up conversations. She had a new boyfriend and seemed to be moving in a serious direction, judging from my daughter's having mentioned him to me on a few occasions. So, I reached out again, said if dude was going to be around for the foreseeable future, I'd like to meet him in person and get on the same page. We set it up, and one day when I went to get the little one, he came out to my car and we chopped it up. Responsible-looking brother. The height of an NBA shooting guard. Bald head. Said he was from down Irvington on the Westside and hooped in his spare time. Offered something like the "She's in good hands with me" line. Then we dapped up, said we'd get together on the court at some point. Neither of us meant it, but it felt polite to pretend we were evolved enough to lower our protective shields in such a way. I went about my day, and some weeks later I was driving a U-Haul to Brooklyn for a new, hopefully fruitful phase of life, feeling like a responsible adult who faced things that made me uncomfortable.

Shit got harder in New York. I had infinite gratitude for being in an environment where the day's agenda solely revolved around exercising my brain about music's significance and social implications. I had gratitude for how I could go into VICE's lobby on a Tuesday afternoon for a glass of water and see Rick Ross coming in for a meeting. And I had gratitude for an international platform to advocate for the music Black people were making in my home state, which I'd never seen accomplished in a comprehensive way before, let alone on that scale. But it was difficult. Every morning started with a FaceTime call from baby girl while she got ready for school. She'd show me her outfit, whatever she was taking for lunch, and then do a little dance. "Oh, that's a nice shirt," I would cheerlead with a grin. When we hung up and said I love you, depending on how well the night before had gone or how demanding of a workday was ahead of me, I was either motivated to go chip away at the prosperous future I promised to myself and everyone else around me or temporarily tormented by how badly I wanted to hug my kid. The evening calls were harder. We would recap her day at school and what we were having for dinner, maybe share another dance move from Triller or help with homework. But sometimes, on rougher days, the evening call was accompanied by a little scrunched-up face with tears rolling down it, snot bubbles coming out of it, and wails leaving from it.

"Daddy, why can't you just live here with me?"

"Daddy has to work here—it won't be like this forever. Okay?"

"But how long?"

"I'm not sure yet. But I'll be there in two more days and we can do whatever you wanna do. Okay? You wanna go to Sky Zone?"

No verbal reply. Just eye rubs and a couple head nods before hanging up. The pain started to transform me, wreck parts of my confidence. I was facing whole Backwoods before going into work daily. Smoking weed wasn't a new habit, but unlike before, I was looking for something more than intensified taste buds and quick laughs. Being in a fog that heavy was a way to coast through the day without emotions getting in the way of my production—the only currency worth a damn at an online culture magazine. My inner dialogue was ruled by comparisons between myself and how my father showed up for me throughout my childhood; how I wasn't upholding his standard. How, even though I was regularly emailing and calling my daughter's teachers, making doctors' appointments, taking her on weekend outings with friends, and ripping up and down the Eastern Seaboard every ten days, it just wasn't good enough. I wasn't good enough.

One night was particularly difficult. Winter was setting in, so the sky was a deep navy by the time I reached home around 6:00 p.m. Brad, one-half of the white couple whose room I was subletting, sat in the living room watching an interview with Donald Trump about his push for the presidency. I sat down on the couch to gather myself, not really paying much mind to the television.

"I'm not talking to my dad right now," Brad blurted out.

I didn't care, but the way he set up the announcement was as if he wanted me to ask why. "Oh yeah?"

Satisfied with my unenthused inquiry, he elaborated, "Yeah. He's a Trump supporter and he won't budge on it. So I told him I won't communicate with him until that changes."

From what it seemed, Brad wanted me to salute him for his bravery, for his attempt at helping dismantle the racist system we're ruled under. Or some shit like that. But I was exhausted by the performance, dealing with my own parent-child obstacles, and, unfortunately for him, not moved by his story. I wished his situation well and went into my furnitureless room.

The phone rang. It was my daughter FaceTiming me. A smile formed in the corner of my mouth. But when I picked up, she was sobbing uncontrollably. Harder than ever before. The curl in my mouth straightened back out. "Dad, why can't you live here with me?" Her eyes were overflowing. I looked at her through the screen, chin up, and delivered what was becoming my go-to. "I'm here for work. I know it's hard, but it won't be this hard forever. I'll see you in a couple days." An attempt at handling it sensibly.

The second we hung up, I sat alone in that furnitureless room on top of that bed-frame-less mattress, lowered my forehead into my palms, and let out a cry that I'd been holding in since I drove that U-Haul up I-95 two months earlier. A cry so delicious in its intensity it moves you through the particular misfortune at hand to misfortunes from your past that were too difficult to deal with at the time, so you make up for them in this moment. What use was finally getting to materialize a dream if the cost of it was having something that brought so much joy be twisted into a source of agony? The guilt of separation found its way into my romantic relationships and friendships; giving my all to anything else felt like a betrayal of my parental priorities.

The yearning, tearful episodes would continue, but they eased up. I cried some more on that bed-frame-less mattress on bad days, but that eased up, too. The daily morning and evening check-ins with my daughter continued, but new and frustrating surprises emerged. I took a walk one night, and while we were on the phone, she mentioned that her mom's boyfriend—the brother

I'd just looked in the eyes and shaken hands with to establish respect a couple months before—told her, if she wanted, she could call him Dad. Already on shaky ground, I lost it. Told her, you can call him Mr. Whatever His Name Is, but he ain't your father and ain't never gonna be your father. And why the fuck is he saying that to you? She didn't have the answers, of course. She was six. I called and texted her mother. Asked what the fuck was going on, wassup with this nigga, and what she had to say about it. Her response—sensible or combative—wouldn't have mattered. My anger was so pronounced, I have trouble remembering much of anything else from that day. Or that week. I just know from that day forward, I had an enemy.

I was less hung up on the suggestion itself but, rather, offended someone could be delusional enough to think that, within months, they were deserving of the same distinction as me. Where was this nigga when I was nineteen years old, explaining to my family that, less than a year after me coming back to Baltimore from college, I was expecting a child? Where was he when I steered through that emotional tumult? Where was this nigga when I was working three jobs at once as a twenty-two-year-old trying to feed that child? Where was he when I was dedicating every ounce of my free time from that child to sharpen my craft and show my face in the corniest places known to man so I could establish a career to sustain myself for that child? Where was this nigga when I was sitting in a furnitureless room on a bed-frameless mattress crying because I missed that child? And why did this nigga wait for me to leave town before deciding he wanted to be called Dad behind my back? Why did he look me in the eyes and shake my hand, then turn around and disrespect me?

The acute anger and resentment for an encroaching male's presence was familiar: I'd grown up feeling it with my own stepfather. And I was comfortable wallowing in that type of contempt. I vowed to mine from the emotional disdain I'd reserved for my stepfather during childhood and to never crawl out of it, as far as dude was concerned. Whenever we saw each other from that point forward, we rarely acknowledged each other's existence. When he was mentioned to me in conversation, I sneered. Made my venom for him known to everyone around me to make sure they were on board, too. At my daughter's eighth birthday party—the last time a collective effort by both parents was made to celebrate her— we planted ourselves at opposite ends of the room, emphasizing the incongruity between us. In those moments, I prepared (and often plotted) for potential avenues for violence to take place. I wished for him to say something out of pocket to me so we could settle our grievances physically. I called up homeboys and family to lay out how we'd get up with him if it ever came down to it: sit outside his house in a car he wouldn't recognize, at that sweet spot of the night when niggas leave out to run random errands, block him in when he's pulling out of a parking space, and then go to work. How far was too far? We hadn't decided.

The preparation was exhilarating when I was in the company of others, but in solitude, I felt its spiritual ramifications. Without realizing it, over the years I've neatly fed myself back through the cycle in which I was raised. So possessed by anger that I've been bypassing boundaries that aren't easily reconstructed. You would think I might know better.

I was around seven years old when I was introduced to my own stepfather, maybe a year or two before he and my mother were married. He had a stern face, with a strong voice that came from his throat rather than his chest, and he operated with a type of stoicism that I'd never experienced before. Conversation didn't appear to be of any real importance to him. He greeted me, and everyone else, with grunts and half-spoken words and typically only communicated instructions on what I could be doing around the house. On the rare occasion that I rode in his car, he never played any music and didn't talk. The only time I detected any nonauthoritative aspects of his personality was away from the crib, when I briefly played for the soccer program he coached in Clifton Park. On the field, he was passionate about the game and much looser in his body language. When he wasn't guiding us on how to be better, he was laughing and shooting the shit with his friends (our other coaches), who, like him, had ended up in Maryland when they left their homes in Jamaica in the eighties and nineties. But those kinds of moments were sparse. On most days, for the bulk of my preadult life, if we spoke at all, it felt like an inconvenient formality, delivered in such a dispirited manner from both sides that silence was often the better option. This stiff, rigid style of interaction, especially as I began to come into my teens, graduated from a constant discomfort to an overflow of resentment.

Like my daughter, I spent my childhood zigzagging between households: my mother's on Tuesdays and Thursdays, my father's on Mondays and Wednesdays, weekends alternating between the two, and touching base at both grandmothers' houses on what felt like daily. A consistently fractured existence that I still can't seem to escape, even as a parent. At my father's house, a discomfort similar to what I experienced at my mother's was the norm.

A specific order needed to be maintained over there. Beds were to be made to hotel-like perfection and sprayed with Lysol as soon as you woke up. After homework was completed, there were extra assignments to keep me sharp: handwriting exercises, math problems, spelling quizzes. Dinner was rarely eaten later than sunset. And like my stepfather, my actual pops never listened to music in the car unless I requested. Without the reassurance of a soft, feminine presence around, I experienced a more active fear at my father's house. His wrath—tragically short-fused—knew few bounds from what I could see. He got into explosive road-rage incidents, once getting out at a light and kicking a man's car for not moving the way he thought the man should. After I got into a scuffle in seventh grade, he came to my school and threatened to jump across my administrator Mr. Ruffin's desk for talking to him sideways. School police escorted us both from the building that day. Even the sound of his keys unlocking the door of my grandmother Bert's house on a day a teacher called home about me acting up sent shocks to my core. Rage was always a possibility with him. But it was balanced by an undeniable love that he expressed for me in his own ways: a consoling conversation after scolding me, the occasional one-on-one basketball game on his parking pad, an excruciatingly corny joke to break the stillness of a room. That type of balance was missing with the male figure at my mother's.

By the time I was in my early teens, my tolerance for the dynamics of my mother's household started to wear thin. I developed a piercing dislike for my stepfather, who, by then, I towered over. Our communication never improved; rather, our interactions with each other became a fixed ambivalence. I grew angry with my mother for allowing it to be this way—a forced joining of pieces that just didn't fit together. From what I could see, she didn't demand any sort of change, and I was desperately craving some. I began fantasizing about what it would take to orchestrate a physical battle between my real father and my mother's husband. I'd already been witness to the violence my father was capable of and figured, if I could convince him, he might deploy that wrath onto the man I desperately wanted out of my life. But my chances were slim to none. As far as I knew, the two had no real experience with each other. Whenever I did mention something about the discomfort I was feeling, my father shrugged it off—said that there was no need for communication unless I was being put in harm's way. He didn't detect a real threat. My stepfather never spoke of my father except in backhanded instances when it was just us two in the house. "You do this at your father's?"—gesturing toward the basketball hoop on the back of my bedroom door. When I answered yes, he countered, "Well, do it there, not here." There was light tension, but it was only expressed with the kind of unbothered dismissal that men use to signal their superiority.

Things were further complicated by the nature of my parents' contentious relationship throughout my childhood. Married while I was in the womb, but broken up before I could crawl, their history was too heavy. If they were in the same space, they rarely acknowledged each other. My father spoke of my mother with an air of disregard, bordering on revulsion. My mother referred to my father as an emotionally unstable aggressor. Both had family members that supported their claims. Neither seemed aware of how my place within the middle of this segregated homelife was disorienting beyond my ability to articulate. So, as the likelihood of an actual solution or brawl between the two old men lessened, my desire to be defended shifted to wanting a reason to physically engage with my stepfather on my own. Whenever he and my mother got into arguments, I wished for him to threaten her with violence so I could rescue her with deadly force. My young, male mind was already conjuring up ways to use a woman as bait in my struggles for power. But it never got to that point. And I probably wouldn't have succeeded if given the chance. As I ran out of ideas, my spirit settled for what constrained people have leaned on throughout history—the consolation of dreaming.

In a series of recurring night visions, the stage would be set like this: I'm home at my mother's and see my stepfather somewhere downstairs, probably in the kitchen, a space so narrow that our bodies are naturally at odds. We weave around each other to open cabinets and the fridge in an attempt to bypass contact. He's grabbing saltines, cheese, and grapes. I'm filling a cup to its brim with dry Cinnamon Toast Crunch. Neither of us speak or initiate eye contact, but he can't pass up the opportunity to eventually offer a critique. Maybe I left an unwashed cup in the sink last night or came into the house too late for his liking. Whatever it is, I'm not trying to hear it no more. Hit him with something like "Man, get the fuck out my face with all that." And before he gets a chance to fix his mouth for a rebuttal, I strike him with the strongest right hook my body is capable of. Unprepared, he falls back and stumbles into the back door. I hit him with more. Left. Left. Right. With every strike I lay down on him, dopamine hits my body and hugs me like warm tea at night. I don't want it to end. When I finally do wake up, for a few seconds, my body still isn't sure what side of my consciousness it's on as I lie there gasping for air. I'd exhaust so much psychological energy fighting to be loved in the dreamworld that I'd need time to physically recover in the material one.

The same confusion and discomfort I felt as a child navigating my stepfather's presence and my parents' unfiltered disdain for each other I've seen on my own kid's face when I dismissed stories she shared about family outings she's had on her mom's side or pushed aside a funny comment her stepfather said. I'd been quicker to fortify the division than to quell her uneasiness on the subject. Felt like my self-respect and manhood were in need of that bolstering, rather than my own child's emotional safety. In that respect, I'm no better than Porter or Malcolm, characters from a film called *Bruiser* that I watched in bed with my lady a little after lockdown ended.

The film was fed to us through Hulu's algorithm on a sleepy spring afternoon—a project that, on the surface, is about the perils of Black boyhood. It's directed by Miles Warren, a young Black man from New York City who, when *Bruiser* came out, was just twenty-five years old. Starring Trevante Rhodes (of *Moonlight* fame) as Porter, Canadian actor Shamier Anderson as Malcolm, and Jalyn Hall as Darious, the story takes place in the present day, on the outskirts of Mobile, Alabama. In its opening scenes, Darious, who just finished his seventh-grade year at an uppity boarding school in town, aimlessly frolics around the plush woods with friends he hasn't seen since the last holiday break, accompanied by rural symphonies of birdcalls and cricket chirps. One day, as boys do around that age, he gets into a tussle with an older kid named Mike and has his lip busted. Trying to quell his anger, he wanders off deeper into the woods, where he runs into a strange man with the physique of an NFL player who rocks combat boots and a forest-green jumpsuit. After some small talk where the man gives Darious pointers on how to properly defend himself, this man realizes the boy is his childhood friend Malcolm's son. It's a truth that seems to defeat him—for a split second, he lowers his head in what appears to be shame.

At home, Darious's parents, Malcolm and Monica, catch wind of the fight with Mike from earlier and instruct Darious—against his intuition and hormones—to take his licks on the chin, turn the other cheek, and stay focused on elevating himself as a human being by not partaking in violence. For the next few days, craving to learn what being a man is about, Darious rides his raggedy bike down the way to link up with the man in the woods (Porter) for some guidance. They spar a little for training. "Get your thumbs up. Left. Left. Right. Left. Left. Right," Porter demonstrates with some air punches. It becomes apparent through their subsequent hangout sessions that Darious isn't just looking for a grown-up's permission to fight; he's craving a more free-flowing adult-male camaraderie, not the stern robotic behavior of his father. As we progress through *Bruiser*, the plot twist finally lands. Monica receives a call one day and it's Porter. As far as Monica and Malcolm know, he's been in the wind for about thirteen years after skipping town when Darious was born, but he's planning to replant his roots in Alabama. As it turns out, Porter is Darious's actual father, but Malcolm is the only dad the boy knows, even though he's aware of there not being a biological link. And now that fate brought his son back into his life, Porter is ready to man up and do what's necessary to make good on his parental shortcomings.

The rest of *Bruiser* is spent lasered in on the ways in which

Malcolm and Porter conjure up tactics to up the score on each other, whether that be over possession of Darious's affections or unresolved fractures in their long-standing, entangled relationship. Porter's animosity toward Malcolm leads him to decisions that threaten Darious's security. Even though Porter is supposed to meet Monica and Malcolm at the state fair, he leads them on a paranoid chase while he buys more time to bond with Darious. Malcolm responds with violence, which starts to distort the portraits he's painted of Porter's personality versus his own. Darious's growing relationship with his biological father leads Malcolm to persuade a police officer friend of his to evict Porter from squatting at a house in the woods where Darious first met him. And Porter responds to Malcolm's anger and attempts at parental protection by essentially kidnapping Darious from home in the middle of the night. A wild chase that concludes with Malcolm finally catching up.

The story ends with the two having an uncomfortably intense brawl, which at no point offers any certainty on whether we're witnessing a slow, gruesome death of one of these men, if not both. In their standoff, shirts are ripped, thunderous punches are landed, blood is drawn, pupils are dilated with acute rage, and impassioned yells are seconds away from turning into tears. As Darious manages to escape to the back seat of Malcolm's car, he looks out with stares of shock and fear, but those looks gradually transform into more of disappointment. It becomes glaringly clear to the child that these men aren't fighting for him. There's a lifetime of pain between them.

In what could have been a chance to recognize a divine moment for renewal, for revision, for restoration, it ends up with two men unable to let go of their need to dominate, to assert power over each other and to wrestle with their boyhood traumas. They're so blinded by this battle that they can't realize they're traumatizing a child—a child wanting, more than anything else, to be loved and heard. Porter's insecurity leads to his full-on unraveling. Malcolm's need for control and a constructed image of self-improvement is shaken by Porter's mere presence. Both of their selfishness and commitment to warring with each other at everyone else's expense ends up in the worst-case scenario: a thirteen-year-old having to drive himself home as they rumble through the night in a dark field. Darious is reduced to a pawn, used as human collateral for opposing sides. You would think the worst-case scenario would have been for Malcolm or Porter to kill each other. Or Darious being physically caught in the crossfire of their rage. But those would have been easy, predictable routes for Miles Warren to take as a filmmaker. Creating a scenario in which a child with three parental figures still has to emotionally fend for himself is the kind of tragedy that stays for a lifetime and grows into smaller tragedies that replay themselves. Even long after the perpetrators are gone.

As I watched this drama unfold in my first viewing, it resonated so deeply that I began to squirm in my bed, looking over to my partner out of the corner of my bad eye to see if she could detect my discomfort. In *Bruiser*, I couldn't help but see myself, my daughter's stepfather, and my own stepfather from my childhood days. Effective filmmaking—or any kind of art making—doesn't set out to make each person who absorbs it feel one particular way. It weaves multiple realities happening simultaneously into focus so that whatever is supposed to find you, will. There are ways that I've felt like Porter in this film, though I've never gone an extended period without seeing my kid or feeling so inadequate that I put her life in danger for my own ego. But, I do know what it feels like to want her all for myself. There are ways that I've felt like Malcolm, busting my ass trying to create a stable life for my kid, even though I have fallen short many times. Warren pulls at those strings incredibly.

Given its intense and accurate emotional presentation, I found it interesting that the inspiration for the film wasn't linked to Warren having a shared experience with Darious. At least that's not what he has revealed in interviews about the project. Warren's light-bulb moment came to him in college when he was browsing through compilations of fight videos from WorldStarHipHop, a phenomenon from the 2010s that was equal parts shameful and arresting. As social media became more of an extension of people's lives, videos of violent altercations at schools, sporting events, and concerts started getting uploaded to the internet for entertainment on what felt like daily; a badge of honor for the victors and a permanent stain on the reputation of the defeated. The main draw of a WorldStar fight video relied on what information was withheld from its viewer. They usually went like this: An opening frame shows two people (mainly boys and men) sizing each other up, surrounded by a group egging them on while they must compute, within seconds, what their first move will be. One swings and misses but recovers quickly. He takes another quick jab and barely lands it on his opponent's chin. Some *Mmmm!*'s from the instigators add fuel. But the other dude counters with a strong hook to the side of the aggressor's face. And as the brother is stunned by the shot, the one who threw the hook grabs him around the waist from behind, bends his knees, and tosses him on the back of his neck. You, behind a laptop screen, wince at the potential of fatal injury, but can't look away. It's too intoxicating to refuse. "Fuck!" somebody yells. It appears to be over. Then, the person recording walks over closer to confirm the fight is over. A close-up shows the fallen brother writhing in pain. He's done. Once the defeat is clear, the onlookers yell in unison, *"World-Starrrrrr!"* And it ends.

You never find out why the fight happened. You rarely find out who was initially in the wrong. The person you find yourself rooting for could have done some irredeemable shit, but that's not why you're there. You're there solely to live vicariously through the masculine desire for combat. The consequences of watching people brutalized for recreation rarely even come to mind. But the mystery behind it all allows you to craft a dramatic narrative in your head. What Warren does masterfully with *Bruiser* is take the time to construct the life events that lead to the high-stakes, out-in-the-open battle we see developing throughout. Under his direction, we're able to see the bottled-up resentment, the unresolved childhood trauma, and the pursuit of self-respect that lead a man to use destruction as a solution. It's likely never the desire to enact indiscriminate brutality.

Two years before *Bruiser* was released as a feature-length film, Warren made a short under the same name where the World-Star inspiration was overt rather than implied. The short starts by stitching together freeze-frames from assorted compilation fight videos with audio from onlookers soundtracking them. Then, the story unfolds showing Darious, played by a different actor, embarrassed and insecure about the reputation his short-fused father has made for himself in their community. Unwilling to accept or adjust his behavior, the father takes issue with people treating him like a burden and ends up proving them right by confronting the father of Darious's friend at a bowling party who doesn't want him in attendance. In an attempt to defend his character, Darious's father ends up falling victim to his own pride and starts a fight with the friend's dad in the middle of a lane. Blood is drawn, and Darious's father's tainted reputation remains intact. Days later, when Darious is playing video games with friends, one discovers a video of the fight circulating online. There's no context attached in this rendering of the event. Just a blurry immortalization of Darious's father initiating force in the interest of preserving his manhood and respect. A young, white compadre of Darious's watches gleefully and smiles before offering a coronation: "Your dad's a legend, bro." But Darious can't see it that way. All he feels when he looks at that video and the smiles on his friends' faces as they build a fantastical narrative around the carnage on their screens is the continued pain, confusion, and frustration of always coming in second place to his father's refusal to consider anyone but the little insecure man inside him.

I don't want to be like Darious's father in either rendition of *Bruiser*. I don't want to be like anyone who's unable to take a long, hard look in the mirror and recognize when they're on some bullshit, or when it's time to move past a situation that brings you nothing but ill feelings. The film was, for me, a moment of revelation. Striking me the way it did, it made me paranoid that my emotional reaction to what I saw could no longer hide behind the mask I held up. It made me want to get a firmer handle on what vexed me. Whether it be my inner child navigating the uncertainty I feel around my stepfather or wanting to sit in the disdain for my daughter's stepfather, neither has done me much good. Both relationships can be managed without the presence of anger. If it was left up to me, *Bruiser* wouldn't be the cultural product that feels the closest to my own experiences. I'd want my association with those aspects of life to feel more like "Color Him Father," the 1969 song by DC soul group The Winstons, which features some of the most earnest and sincere crooning about a stepfather who showered his stepchildren with love, useful advice, and reassurance. That isn't the case for me, but it can still be the case for my kid, which is a future I can try to facilitate. I'd rather it be that reality than one that causes decades-long affliction.

THE EXCHANGE

THERE'S A RITUAL I'VE developed with my daughter, Ayden, over the past few years that brings us to a closer understanding of each other. The practice requires us to offer—or withhold—the stamp of approval for what music each of us is currently listening to. Doesn't have to be anything new, just what's occupying space in the rotation. It's dictated by the length of car rides we take. If we're just running a quick errand, like going to get snowballs in the warmer months, the rule is that we go song for song. When I'm headed to drop her off at school, which takes about thirty minutes, we get a few at a time, say about three each. And when we're taking longer road trips, like from Baltimore to New York City, you're allowed to control the vibes for a good twenty minutes at a time. Now that she's a year away from starting her high school career, I find that it's one of the more useful tools for keeping a constant stream of conversation going. You ask a kid in eighth grade how school went that day and, barring a cataclysmic event, good luck on getting anything more detailed than "Fine," "Cool," or "It was okay." But having an open forum about why she thinks the songs I played from MIKE's *Disco!* album are unlistenable is how you get to the root of something.

On a recent drive from her cheerleading practice, she played a couple tracks from a group of kids out of Philly who, since 2020, have breathed new life into the East Coast club music scene: "Get Humpy" by Bril and 5 Star, "2Humpy Anthem" by 2Rare and 2Humpy, and "Buckle Up" by PGS Spence of the Philly Goats. During the pandemic, this new crop of artists built on a natural progression of cross-pollination that'd been happening in the genre for years. Now, with the dominance of TikTok for people born in the new millennium, bite-size tracks with accompanying dances get the most traction, which is where Philly made their latest mark.

Club music has gone through quite a few changes in its thirty-_plus years of existence. Once the club capital transitioned from Baltimore to North Jersey, it started to interact with what was happening in the New York tristate area. In the late 2010s, New York rappers developed their own take on drill music coming out of the UK, effectively changing their flow patterns to more of a stuttering choppiness. Jersey rappers, because of their proximity to NYC, adopted this style of rapping, but instead of using drill beats, decided to rap over Jersey Club. Then, the movement shifted one metro area south to Philadelphia, where the rappers carved their own way of rapping over club beats. My first fatherly inclination was to dismiss what Ayden queued up, to mention how all club music originates from Baltimore and will never surpass its glory days from my teenage years in the late 2000s. But then I remembered that I'm supposed to be a music critic, someone who's up to speed on what's happening sonically in all corners of Black America. "This is pretty cool, I guess. The lyrics suck, but it's cool," I tease.

"They don't suck, Dad. This is what people are doing on Tik-Tok," Ayden snaps back.

I try my best to let these cultural exchanges remain free of restrictions. If the lyrics to songs get a little too suggestive, I'll give her a "Come on now. This is a bit much." And that's so much of music right now. If it isn't explicitly sexual, it's extolling the murderous appetite of young men whose social currency hinges on how violent they are. Right now, within her friend group of middle schoolers in Baltimore County, the hottest local collective of artists are Mg Shorty, Mg BabyK, and Lor Mark, all of whom are trying their hardest to bring drill sensibilities to the Baltimore rap scene. It's something the city has never fully embraced. In terms of production, like most rappers in Baltimore they like to flow over a bastardized version of Atlanta trap beats, the type of stuff you'd hear Lil Baby rap on. But, in lyrical content, they rarely part their lips to gloat about anything other than the many ways they'd like to wreak havoc on people—often to the extent of death. When it's her turn to control the music and she plays them, not only do I make it a point to underline how mediocre I find it, but also how important it is for her to understand that, while it might be on trend, there's something intrinsically wrong with carrying on this way. And she's quick to defend her selection: "But, Dad, some of the music you play isn't that much different." It's a reality check I need to hear. The difficulty in parsing through the many regional rap scenes throughout the country right now is that many of the most popular artists utilizing the most interesting, chaotically futuristic-sounding productions are rapping about killing people with the matter-of-factness of talking about what kind of shoes they're wearing. As I get older—now in my mid-thirties—it's getting increasingly more difficult to reconcile with this truth. It's also a challenge when your kid who's twenty years younger than you is effectively absorbing much of the same content as you on social media. What would it say about me if I continue to unconsciously celebrate or platform artists I don't even want my daughter listening to? It's one of the more pressing dilemmas I'm facing today.

When Ayden was a small child, one of the biggest pleasures of parenthood, for me, was that I was able to mold her musical taste into whatever I thought was best—what would make her into the most well-rounded and cultured baby girl you ever met. She entered this world in the fall of 2010, and for the first few months of her life, Kanye West's *My Beautiful Dark Twisted Fantasy* occupied the most audible space in my '06 Altima, but at that stage of her development I never had to consider Chris Rock talking about reupholstered pussy on "Blame Game" or the plethora of twisted shit Kanye rapped about. By the time she reached the toddler stage and began attempting to recite what I was playing, I felt a great sense of responsibility wash over me. *What will create an enriching musical experience for her?* I thought. Ridiculous as it might have been, I got strict about the testy content and veered off into what I found more appropriate: Adele, Gnarls Barkley, Bob Marley, Gil Scott-Heron—music that had the potential to broaden her sonic references.

She loved Bob, especially. By the time she was two years old, somehow, she could parrot every word to "Smile Jamaica," "Natty Dread," and "War," and would even start crying and throwing fits if I didn't let them run on an infinite loop in the car when we were headed to day care or home. At home, I'd queue up videos

of Bob's performances on YouTube and she'd stand there atten-
tively watching his every move. Within a week's time, she'd have
the whole routine memorized. Life knew no better joy than those
moments at that time. The sunny Saturday mornings of my own
childhood were soundtracked by my mother blasting classics
from Marley, Beres Hammond, and Buju Banton out of her beat-up
Volkswagen Golf or around the house while she cleaned. Passing
that tradition down to Ayden went from an attempt to expand her
musical intake to an act of preserving family traditions.

From Bob, Ayden moved on to wanting to hear Damian's "The
Master Has Come Back" and Buju Banton's "Wanna Be Loved"
repeated infinitely. Eventually, reggae worked its way out of her
purview. From there, she developed an obsession with Kelela's
Cut 4 Me album, which stayed in my rotation for a few years. One
of my fondest memories that's immortalized by video evidence
is taking her to Brooklyn's Afropunk in 2015, where Kelela performed. In the front-facing video, a four-year-old Ayden sits on
my shoulders, absolutely fixated on the performance and swaying her upper body back and forth while she sang the album's title
track in unison along with the crowd. My direct influence on her
intake ended shortly thereafter, right around the time she began
school. Soon, she'd be teaching me.

During the pandemic, on evenings when it was time to unplug
from screens—emails and Zoom calls for me, and Zoom schooling for her—we'd eat dinner in the TV room while Ayden granted
me the privilege of watching her browse YouTube. Sometimes
we watched Unghetto Mathieu, a twenty-one-year-old from
Georgia who tested whether people's diamond jewelry was fake
at the Lenox Square mall in Atlanta. Sometimes we looked at

Dhar Mann, a filmmaker who made feel-good short films meant to encourage people to be decent to one another. But the channel with the tightest grip on Ayden around then was Anna Oop, a gossip channel in the tradition of *TMZ* or *The Wendy Williams Show*, but solely focused on the drama of adolescent TikTokers. Anna had no face but had millions of subscribers, and she delivered news from behind the image of an animated teenage white girl with two blond buns and running eyeliner. Ayden first started watching the show when lockdowns were implemented; it popped up through her algorithm, probably as a result of her bouncing between TikTok compilations and *Dance Moms* reruns.

The flow of the show was perfect for its young audience's need for constant multimedia stimulation, and likely the only thing that occupied Ayden enough to watch it with her phone down. Every few seconds, Anna showed flashes from TikTokers' dances to clips of their IG Live streams to stock footage to viral reaction clips from other parts of the internet. With her unbothered whine of a voice, she pulled viewers into the young TikTokers' world: *Tony Lopez is being accused of coercing underage girls into sexual acts! DaBaby is using JoJo Siwa as a punch line in a new song! Charli D'Amelio isn't crediting Black creators whose dances she copies!* The theatrics made me recoil, feeling embarrassment for watching and a discomfort around gaining more insight into what my kid was absorbing without me knowing. It was also a perfect primer on how Black culture—more specifically, Black LGBT culture— gets co-opted and repurposed as universal "internet" culture. Anna Oop's channel name riffs on Jasmine Masters's "And I Oop" moment in 2015; Masters is a highly visible drag performer who captured widespread fanfare after being a cast member on the seventh season of *RuPaul's Drag Race*. The tea Anna serves was mostly associated with young white TikTokers, but she regularly accentuated her speech with a drawn-out *gurrrrl* she learned from Black people.

The first few times I watched the series, I was equal parts annoyed and troubled. I didn't want my ten-year-old Black daughter, who has grown up in majority-Black Baltimore her whole life, surrounded by people who culturally affirm her, to be swayed into comparing herself to a curated, whitewashed image of what success, visibility, and value looks like for a young person—especially when that success is based on a watered-down version of her own culture. But because she doesn't know a world where Black culture is just for Black people—something that last felt true during my adolescent years in the 2000s—she met my frustrations with amused dismissal. Those bonding moments, when I'm allowed a front seat in her orbit of entertainment, gave me a chance to reflect. When I was around her age, I had a similar curiosity about what was happening in the white world that didn't have any real proximity to my experience. *MTV News* and Howard Stern's show on *E!* gave me those voyeuristic opportunities to learn and to be entertained, and even in elementary school I was sharp enough to grasp those programs as not being much more than something to pass the time. They had no bearing on my self-worth. I made the unfair assumption that my kid doesn't have the agency to be able to distinguish entertainment from indoctrination. In a lot of ways, it felt as if Anna Oop was Ayden's first taste of having something catered just to her interests, something that doesn't overlap with what I, her mother, or other family members were into. But even the things she pays the most attention to these days are treated with nonchalance. When I asked about her fascination with Anna, she gave an unbothered explanation for her newfound obsession: "Because it's tea. I don't really care about the people she's talking about. The people are always in drama all the time, and it's funny."

These days, I'm lucky if she even wants to share the things that she feels are just catered to her and her friend group. Now when we lounge around the house, *Catfish* reruns and true crime documentaries are her go-to. But also, as much as I was annoyed by Anna Oop's existence, it was probably the last form of cultural production she's latched on to that is actually geared toward an adolescent audience. Everything she absorbs now is something that people in their twenties are also absorbing—and it scares the hell out of me. Because now that I'm in my thirties, whatever I pass along to her—even though I'm convinced it's cool by all worthwhile metrics—is automatically diminished in value, at least while she's in my company. Kelela isn't cool anymore, artists like the Nigerian superstars Rema and Asake aren't cool, any rap I listen to that isn't about blowing someone's head off is automatically uncool. And whatever music or art from my generation she does find and deem cool, somehow, once she grasps it, it doesn't belong to me anymore.

In the early spring of 2024, we went to a Drake concert at Long Island's UBS Arena in New York, just a week after Kendrick threw the punch that started their historic battle. For someone I've been listening to before Ayden was even born, Drake has kept himself afloat in the pop culture sphere longer than any of his rap peers. The key to his longevity, I think, is that the Canadian megastar has masterfully calculated whom he can connect himself with to remain relevant. Ayden and I have been going to concerts, festivals, and local music shows since she was a small child, but this time, her excitement is that she's going to see artists who have elevated cultural currency in her friend group. The tour's opener was Chicago rapper Lil Durk, who, even though he's just two years younger than me, has a vise grip on youth culture. It's he whom Ayden has been talking about seeing the week leading up to the show. "He's just so inspirational" was a recurring talking point for her.

When we arrived to the show, Durk was about halfway through the set and her eyes were lit up like she was seeing a once-in-a-lifetime artist, jumping up and down, never giving her phone a break from recording. The wildly popular social media comedian Druski—whom kids would probably equate to the significance of a modern-day Bernie Mac—was in attendance, helping fill in space between performances. Once Drake came out, a resounding collective scream came from the crowd, and he performed for what had to be ninety minutes. I looked over at Ayden, rapping every single word with supreme passion. From "Nonstop" to "God's Plan" to "First Person Shooter," she and a sea of other young people born after 2000 basked in the air of megastardom—excited in a way that I just couldn't be after already enduring his better years and embarrassing mishaps. For an artist like Drake to continue breaking chart records, selling out tours like this, and occupying mental space in the cultural zeitgeist, thirty-four-year-old me's fandom is expendable. But in that moment, surveying the stadium, I thought, *This all belongs to her now.*

WELCOME HOME

DECEMBER 2017

THE DAY BEFORE NEW Year's Eve 2017, I was perched atop Constitution Hill in Johannesburg, South Africa, desperately fighting back tears. I was at the first Afropunk to ever take place on the Motherland, and the woman hosting the festival had just yelled "Welcome home!" to all the Black Americans in attendance. I did not want to cry in that moment because, intellectually, I know that the Africans who were transported to the United States, Caribbean islands, and South America hundreds of years ago did not, in any considerable amount, come from this part of Africa but, rather, the West and Central regions. And I also follow enough people on Twitter from the Continent who frown upon the diasporans that fall for these emotional gestures, citing our proclivity to seek out anemoia rather than engaging with the present-day realities our distant relatives endure. But I am not a robot, and what actually *would* have been corny is if I stood there, eight thousand miles from home, acting like standing on African soil was anything less than a miracle for a Black American. Shit, standing on any soil outside the western hemisphere is a miracle for most niggas I know. I blinked twice to release one tear, but stopped it before it rolled down my cheek to maintain an illusion of dignity.

I ended up in Johannesburg by convincing the higher-ups at VICE to send their staff writer for the music section (me) across the world to cover this event. I urged that an event founded in Brooklyn making its way to the Continent signaled the potential for negroes of my generation to establish alliances with young Black people halfway across the world. Young Black people whose nation, like ours, exposed them to centuries of racialized violence and subjugation at the hands of Europeans. There was some truth to that: out of all African folks, South Africans, from a societal standpoint, do have the most in common with Black Americans. They are the only ones on this landmass who constantly interact with white people at every level of society. They lived through state-sanctioned segregation that, in effect, is still alive and well, but which just exists in a more covert manner. And their African-ness—due to the effects of their oppression, in relation to their behavior and customs—is constantly being questioned by other Africans. But the truth was, while this all factored in, I really wanted to travel outside America for the first time, and figured that to accomplish that I needed to construct a narrative around me yearning to find my roots. Luckily, after scrambling to put a pitch together where I identified some artists doing great work in SA, the plan worked, and my request was approved with relative ease. VICE was at its apex, feverishly spanning the globe to establish itself as the new worldwide media power. The company had been sending people across the map regularly since I started the previous year, so I knew it was worth taking a shot.

Afropunk's arrival to these shores had been divisive. For one, the festival wasn't very punk anymore and hadn't been for a few years. The artists the organizers booked then and continue to book now could perform at any well-known festival around the world, more or less. The only thing alternative about most of the artists was their fashion sense, and even that's up for debate. Alternative or punk, in the eyes of many in the present era, is more closely associated with a look rather than an attitude, sound, or a set of politics. You could make the most conventional brand of R&B, rap, or house music, but if you have face tattoos, an interesting hairdo, and wear custom-made clothes, you're automatically *other*. Not that this evolution particularly bothers me; someone would be well within their rights to question if I'm representative of the festival's initial audience. But, anytime a company, group, or individual transitions from counterculture to mainstream, questions of validity will follow. Secondly, Constitution Hill, where the festival was being held, was previously the site of a women's prison in which Black inmates (including anti-apartheid activists) were segregated from the whites and subjected to a heightened level of punishment. Lastly, the number of South African artists on the bill, according to people I spoke to there, was embarrassingly low. The headlining act was American singer Anderson .Paak.

Still, most of the people I talked to on the ground were happy that Afropunk had landed there, regardless of the conditions. They'd been following the festival on social media since its inception in Brooklyn and were eager for the chance to be photographed in outfits they spent weeks putting together. While there, I observed looks ranging from earth-toned body armor to hair decorations that resembled red clay and clocked some of the shiniest gold jewelry I've ever seen on human beings. I was happy to be there, too, if for nothing other than the opportunity to people-watch and to begin figuring out what aspects of my identity were undoubtedly African—a tough call to make, since few Africans on this planet have been able to exist independent of encroachment from outside forces.

As emotional as that moment was, the highlight of my day wasn't being welcomed back home. It was when a young woman approached me, complimented me on my beauty, and asked if I'd traveled from Ghana, due to my facial features and the richness of my dark skin. Before that interaction, I'd never had someone point me toward a specific nation of origin based on my appearance. That's not something we're intrinsically capable of in the States. But to have someone on this side of the world do it offered an assuredness that an ancestry test just can't. All day, I'd been falling into the sentimentality I'd hoped to avoid, but the energy was too rich, too good-natured, to act unfazed. This was a moment that allowed me to quiet some internal storms, feelings of being a distant African of unspecified origin. I was closer to whatever answers I was seeking.

The first two days I experienced of Afropunk were full of that type of warmth and good nature. After one set, I was tipped to go to an after-hours spot called Kitcheners in the Braamfontein neighborhood, a beautiful cerulean Creole town-house structure, similar to what you would see in New Orleans's French Quarter. A crowd of young, well-dressed socialites seamlessly flowed from the front of the venue into its open floor plan inside. Some danced lightly to the pulsating rhythms of gqom, the country's addictive, pounding iteration of house music, which inspires a fresh crop of dances on what feels like weekly, based on my Instagram feed. To me, it's the transatlantic cousin of Baltimore Club, similar in innovative foundation, but raised different due to one coming out of small row houses and the other out of township shacks. Others at the function hugged, laughed, and huddled around one another, drinks in hand. Visually, the mixture of folks—racially and stylistically—didn't feel much different from a night out in Brooklyn.

I sipped a cognac-and-ginger-beer concoction while a friend who lives and works in Joburg introduced me to his peers; nothing more elaborate than small talk, smiles, and having to embarrassingly answer, "The States," each time I was asked where I was visiting from. In America, I don't completely identify with my Americanness. Most of Black people's existence in America feels more akin to being leftover captives of war rather than actual citizens. But you can't tell that to a non-American person who doesn't have the proper context and can sniff the Red, White & Blue out of you from across the room in your posture, mannerisms, and delusional separation from reality. Away from the States, you're forced to accept your branding or be made a fool of. I was quick to learn that some South Africans suffer from a similar lack of self-awareness.

The last person my buddy introduced me to was a white woman with a short blond haircut who was a staple in the local music scene for throwing shows and helping artists in the early parts of their careers. I told her I was there to spend time with some artists, hit Afropunk, and try to get sense of what it's like to be a young Black person coming up in South Africa right now. "It's a shame what Afropunk is doing here. They have no idea what's going on and they're interfering with people who've had New

Year's events happening for years," she yelled into my ear over the music within seconds of shaking my hand. "And they say they're here to support young African artists but don't have any white South Africans on the bill."

I raised my head away from her mouth and backed away in bewilderment. "Huh?"

"Yeah. How can you say you're about lifting up artists, but purposely leave off white South Africans? That's weird."

"You know Afropunk is an event dedicated to giving a platform to artists of African descent, right? A white South African ain't of African descent. They come from Europe, no matter how long they've been here."

She paused with her mouth open as if she was unfamiliar with the truth of her origins or had never been challenged to face the reality of being a product of settler colonialism. "Yes, but it's more complex than that," she suggested. "My family isn't rich . . . they came here as poor farmers." I stared back, unmoved. She kept going: "Look, I wish I weren't white. My husband is Black. My children are Black. I work with Black artists. It's a complicated situation." I left her to deal with her existential crisis alone, ordered another drink, and called a car back to my hotel.

The next day, a few hours before the clock sent us into 2018, me and my good friend Shan, who was in Joburg for a women's retreat, got a taxi to a place called the Tennis Club. To my surprise, it wasn't just called that for irony's sake. We pulled up to an actual sporting complex with a tennis court that was accessed through a small winding road that our driver struggled to locate in the dark. When we found the entrance, we were greeted by a young man and a woman who asked whom we were there to see and gestured to the staircase behind them. It was sketchy but in the most delightful way, like we were seconds away from walking into a sex party or an underground gambling ring.

The stairway opened up to a type of skybox suite, with roof-to-floor-length glass windows providing an overhead view of the tennis court. The space was dark, and groups of people—confusingly white preppy-looking types for the most part—were scattered around, drinking and talking. I was looking for Moonchild Sanelly, an artist quickly rising through the ranks as one of gqom's most exciting vocalists. I familiarized myself with her music months before making the trip to Joburg and recognized her as somewhat of a badass of the scene; almost punk in her approach to disruption. Her voice sounds like a rhythmic nasal lullaby weaving through skipping tom drums and backing chants—a good contrast to the genre's deep use of bass. After scanning the room for a few minutes, I spotted her signature blue crochet mushroom hairdo at a booth in the corner and introduced myself. She offered us champagne while going over a setlist with her boyfriend/DJ/manager before rushing into a small room upstairs to take the stage. Moonchild was the one leading the party into 2018. The crowd was a bit more than fifty people, seemingly excited for the New Year, but not in the get-fucked-up-just-because way I've seen people celebrate back home. Meanwhile, I was hyped just to exist in the space, somewhere I didn't imagine myself going just two months before.

Moonchild's music has thematic purpose. Some of her most popular songs deal with the hurdles of being a woman out in the Johannesburg nightlife scene and what women deal with in their intimate relationships. That night, dressed in a plastic see-through dress and fishnet stockings, she performed "F-Boyz," which chronicles her experience digging a guy who claimed to be a high roller, but ended up being a real estate agent who took women to houses he helped sell under the guise of owning them. She then went into her verse on DJ Maphorisa's mega-gqom-hit "Midnight Starring," where she energizes the song by talking about how she hates when her man ignores her posts on social media. People in the packed room raised their champagne glasses, shouted, "Yebo," a Zulu expression of affirmation, and danced exuberantly with their partners. Me and Shan stood in the middle of the floor, smiling in astonishment at how much this gathering felt like the little packed DIY spaces back home that played club music. A reminder that these underground electronic-music sanctuaries are universal in their necessity. "Damn, niggas really in Africa," I said, pulling Shan in for an over-the-shoulder hug.

Moonchild's artistic mission is all about creating and feeding these on-the-fringe communities. Beyond the music, she's helped springboard conversations around sexual liberation for women in South Africa, who she says are often shamed and targeted by men for the free expression they enjoy in places like this. "When it comes to my art, there is no sex that comes with it. It's art," she tells me after her set. "I feel like one of the biggest problems with the hip-hop artists we have here, if you're not sexy and you got bars, you're an L. If you're sexy without the bars, you're hot. So you'll get someone who's hot and translates American songs to South Africa, and that's the winner. So your sexuality limits your greatness." Her refusal to give in to the shallow desires of the market is probably why Moonchild's following is considerably low for an artist of her abilities. But she's found a way to carve out a lane for herself in the alternative spaces that lean more toward majority-white crowds—essentially a mirror of what "off-kilter" Black artists experience in the States and Europe when they don't care to prioritize conventional standards in exchange for opportunities. It wasn't until Moonchild ended up on the last verse of "Midnight Starring" that people started to care on a broad scale, almost a decade into her artistic career. "If you start to base your career off of what men think, you will lose. Right now, I could be raped outside. That's a reality. But I don't live scared," Moonchild said. "You need to reject a pair of dicks first before you get the contract offer. It might just take you a little longer, which is the route I chose because I ain't gon' fuck you. I got talent. Fuck you. I'm the only Black girl and electronic musician in the white spaces that gets respected. I'm only new to the mainstream people."

I needed that conversation to wake me out of my early, reductive expectations in Joburg. In my ignorance, I thought my limited knowledge of South Africa's history as an apartheid state would guide conversations with people who were born into the system. It never even dawned on me that young people in SA were occupied with present-day life. I thought I'd arrive, enjoy the scene, and come home to lay out the ways that people born in the late eighties and early nineties in South Africa were driven by their being the first postapartheid generation, on a mission to get what was taken from their families, especially the creative class. But that just wasn't the case. Reckoning with the history of apartheid is prevalent in South African society from what I'd observed, but considering it had been over since most people I was speaking with were preschool children, if not infants, there are conditions in place that—even if originally caused or accelerated by apartheid—require more immediate attention, like the sexual violence Moonchild focuses on, extreme poverty, and all the ills that come with being relegated to the bottom rung of the social ladder. It was a sign for me to recalibrate my approach to reporting, ensuring that I wasn't predetermining an angle before connecting with actual humans. With these new truths in mind, I continued to undo my American tendency of thinking that having a marginal knowledge of a place and people was equal to understanding the full texture of a lived experience.

The next day, I caught a car to an upscale suburb of the city called Midrand to meet eMTee, a rapper born and raised in Soweto, the biggest township outside of Joburg, whose career has afforded him a way out by age twenty-five. He's the front man of a collective called ATM (African Trap Movement), and his music is, more or less, a carbon copy of what's come from the Black American South. But the magic in eMTee's music is where he distinguishes himself from his American influences, drawing parallels between what he witnessed in Soweto and the world depicted through trap coming from the States. Take his song "Manando," for instance, where he eulogizes a slain childhood friend who looked out for him as a youth. On it, he reminisces about how Manando taught him how to play marimba, protected him from school bullies, and gave him money for haircuts when he was in need. Somewhere along the way, Manando got deep into some shit he couldn't get out of. He was an enforcer in the neighborhood, carrying guns and having police in his back pocket, but ended up going on the run when he got word that people from an opposing side were trying to find him. Unfortunately, while lying low, Manando was shot and lost his life before getting to witness his little man—baby eMTee—blossom into one of South Africa's most important artists of his generation. The immense agony is channeled convincingly through eMTee's melodic stretching of vocals throughout the track. Another song video, "Corner Store," provides visual evidence of the shared conditions of the hood across the Atlantic, as he switches between Zulu and English, showing where he and his friends post up when he returns to his section of Soweto. If he was American, the music itself probably wouldn't be strong enough to hold me, but there's more at stake here—an opportunity to understand the diaspora through lines.

"From my neighborhood, to the schools, we were dissed for liking hip-hop and sagging our pants. People are like, 'What are you doing? You trying to be Migos?'" he told me as we leaned against the island in his kitchen and his homeboy Lucas rolled blunts for the drive we were about to take back to his hood. "I got on the trap wave, and I rolled with it because this shit talks about what we go through, just in a different way. My nigga's auntie not selling dope, but she's selling alcohol. I don't have a trap house, but I got a shack. That's the African Trap Movement." To him, there was no better way to articulate his reality than through rap's newest iteration of street music, but I fear he had taken the influence a little too much to heart—which is often the case when you're duplicating something from a distance.

We packed into eMTee's black Mercedes GLE truck with a handful of ATM members, ready to head back to the neighborhood where he grew up. Finally, I thought, a chance to observe the everyday flow of Black South African life. He clamped onto the steering wheel, backed out his garage, and mashed on the gas until we reached Johannesburg's M1 highway toward Soweto. He accelerated with reckless abandon, periodically reaching toward the back seat to grab a double cup of codeine mixed with Mountain Dew. I couldn't see the speedometer from my seat, but judging from the trees and cars whipping by, we had to have been damn close to the 100 mph mark. With no sign of concern, he started to feel around the overhead console for a new pair of sunglasses, swapping between his dark shades and a pair of circular yellows that complimented his baby blue tee and pink cap. He took a call. I was scared as fuck, but I was playing it cool.

As we entered Soweto, eMTee directed my attention to the view from the car's left side. The scenery had changed so rapidly that I would have missed it if he didn't say anything. "You see those shacks?" He pointed to the multicolored line of barely standing homes in the near distance. "Every time I see those shacks, I get angry. These white folks, man. They done fucked the world up." I nodded in agreement. We exited the M1 and parked outside a nondescript building in his old stomping grounds. It looked like a school or hospital, but up a few flights of stairs and around the back of a building, we arrived at a pop-up shop for the sportswear brand Styla Gang, which is owned by his friends. For the rest of the day, we toured eMTee's hood, and at no point did I feel like I was in unfamiliar territory. The more we walked around, the more I began to see the world depicted through his lyrics.

The corner stores, mostly operated by Somali brothers, were constructed just like the ones I grew up patronizing; only with steel bars separating the store clerk from customers, rather than cloudy bulletproof glass. There was a slither of tension, but also an acceptance of this treatment as customary. During our walk, eMTee and his guys recognized someone from their neighborhood walking by, a guy not much older than us, who was clearly disoriented. They said he was on a drug that's starting to take over the streets there, turning people into zombielike shells of themselves, walking around aimlessly until the high wears off and they need a new fix. I instantly thought of the brothers and sisters back home in Baltimore whom I'd seen slowly shuffling through the streets, plagued by the same sickness. Then we headed to a park where old heads were posted up with their car doors wide open, blasting music. Kids were running around a basketball court. This is what segregation looks like there: extreme levels of disenfranchisement softened by the comfort of community. I can't say it's any different from what I've known most of my life. I think that's the point eMTee is trying to make in his music and by showing me around—that our shared conditions outweigh our distinctions. "Not to sound all political, but they've caged us in South Africa," he said. "A lot of people I know inside those villages, they can't walk to the city. They've taken a certain color of people and put them in these shitty areas." It pained me to say I knew the feeling.

I left South Africa filled with gratitude and energized by having been thousands of miles away from a homeland that was chosen for me by unkind forces and where, at every turn, I encountered young Black people who were eager to extend love and hospitality. We traded stories of what it felt like to live under oppressive systems, what we felt it'd take to dismantle them, and, more important, we acknowledged how good it felt to be in the company of folks who understand exactly how hard it is to maneuver through those obstacles. I can't say I necessarily walked away with any new solutions. But I walked away with confirmation that our experiences aren't singular, thus feelings of loneliness were no longer needed.

DECEMBER 2019

It's eleven days before New Year's Eve 2019, and I'm being reprimanded by police officers on the side of a highway in Lagos, Nigeria. On the way back to my hotel from an event with friends, officers flashed a light into our vehicle as we approached the tollgate to take us into the upscale Lekki area of the city. For whatever reason, once the light hit my face in the passenger seat, we were ordered to get out of the vehicle. My friend Amarachi, who facilitated my stay, advised everyone in the truck to hand over whatever we had in our possession to our driver once she realized we'd be searched. But I've brought my Black American distrust for my fellow brother across the Atlantic and figured if I let the driver know I had weed in my pocket, he might rat me out. Furthermore, if I wanted to access the herb to even hand it over, I couldn't get it; the pockets of the pants I wore were so deep that I couldn't even locate the small container I'd bought from someone earlier that night.

Besides the driver, I'm the only male in my party. I'm joined by Amarachi, Ivie, and Stephanie, who all have the potential to charm officers with their womanly aura and ability to communicate in pidgin. I had neither, so I stayed quiet for my own good. "Take everything out of your pockets," we were ordered. Mine were filled with shit I'd compiled throughout the day: nairas, my passport, ChapStick, wristbands from the event we'd just left, a lighter, and, of course, the weed, which is, to my dismay, miraculously detectable now that I'm standing. Trying to be proactive, I take out everything but the grass, thinking I can get ahead of the officers before they search me. I'm unsuccessful. While my hands are occupied, one pats me down and locates the small container. Even though we're under bright fluorescent streetlights that make the contents of my package visible, he still shines a flashlight onto it and yells, "Ah! He has loud!" Simultaneously, I have an inner laugh about his referring to weed by its outdated pseudonym and a minor panic attack that I might be going to a Nigerian jail on my second night in the country. "You have broken the law," he asserts before confiscating my phone and passport.

In a panic, Amarachi pleads with the officers to let it slide, but they're not in the mood to budge. "He is an American journalist here to report on things happening in Nigeria, and this is unacceptable," she argued. I really wasn't, but I kept quiet, kept my head high, and stared off into the distance, sensing their desire for me to be combative. Amarachi assures me that she'll get me out of this jam and makes a call to a friend whose dad is a former politician of some sort. I'm informed this is how shit works here, especially around Christmas: an influx of first-generation Nigerian Americans or British Nigerians descend upon their homeland, sometimes accompanied by non-Nigerian friends who are visiting for the first time, and are shaken down by local authorities for cash. Apparently, my braids, gold teeth, and tattoos insinuate that I'm either an American or a Yahoo boy—the term used for young Nigerian scammers—and thereby prime for extortion. I mention to Amarachi that I can offer them a few dollars to let us go, but it isn't that simple. My money won't suffice in this situation—it'll need to come from someone with a significant amount of social capital, of which I have zero in this nation.

We wait outside for hours, my brain producing a plethora of

hypothetical scenarios in which I do end up in jail, stripped of my passport and cell phone, cut off from loved ones for an indefinite time. But something tells me if I stay calm and refuse to engage or show any signs of stress, I'll make it out.

After more time passes, the officers are growing impatient and try to call Amarachi's bluff about this former politician coming to sort things out. So, they force the driver to get back in the truck, push me into the back seat, and two of them—full-grown men—try to fit into the passenger seat together. "Take us to the station," they demand. Then, trying to close the door, they nearly break it. Amarachi, Ivie, and Stephanie hop in the back with me. "Y'all aren't taking him anywhere without us." I'm appreciative of their bravery, but grow more worried as time goes on. The officers' guns are the size of an eight-year-old child, and they're irritated.

Just two hours prior, I was having the time of my life at the Hard Rock Cafe, which, in Lagos, doubles as a legit music venue at night, rather than just a shitty tourist trap of a restaurant. I'd been invited here for the annual onslaught of December festivities because, as an editor at *The FADER*, I've made it a priority to platform what's happening in the new, youth-driven Nigerian music scene. Ever since I broke into the New York music media landscape, I had a plan to use my power to connect the dots with as many stops across the Black anglophone world as possible, with the hope of understanding what could bring us together. And to me, the Nigerian music scene contains some of the most interesting art being created in the diaspora. The artists here are somewhere at the intersection of hip-hop, dancehall, Afrobeats, dream pop, and R&B, making a kind of sound that the world has yet to hear. At Hard Rock, the alté scene (short for *alternative*) was front and center, an ecosystem of young Nigerians who are escaping the catchall, mainstream Afrobeats labeling. The country's leading genre, Afrobeats, blends indigenous musical elements with reggae and has megastars like Burna Boy, Wizkid, and Davido. But alté artists—at least the ones at the show—are crafting a world that encompasses more inventive production borrowed, in part, from British electronic subgenres, an avant-garde film approach to music videos, and a fashion sense that pulls from the American Y2K era. And it's not just the music artists who are crucial in this universe; there are streetwear designers, skaters, and visual artists who all contribute to the look and feel of what alté represents.

I was preparing myself to finally see an IRL showcase of the kids from here we'd been covering at *The FADER*. Artists on the bill included Santi, who, earlier in 2019, released an album titled *Mandy & the Jungle*, which gets better as more time passes. The project feels best when listened to from start to finish, as he guides you through a soundscape that borrows from magitek gaming worlds, the vocal textures of Damon Albarn, and flow patterns from nineties dancehall. He was joined by Odunsi the Engine, a crucial figure in this scene, who carries the aura of a Nigerian rockstar by subverting rigid, present-day gender expression and galvanizing the kids who don't live up to conventional popularity. During his set, Odunsi previewed music from his forthcoming EP, *Everything You Heard Is True*, which included a song with a hook that, to the crowd's delight, just repeats "I'm wicked, sexy!" over and over. He ran it back multiple times to optimize audience participation. The two were also joined by their buddies Deto Black, a young fashionista who raps as if she doesn't care about rapping, which is kind of her whole appeal, and a guy named Maison2500, whose music flagrantly copies Playboi Carti, but since no one seemed to take issue with it, it works perfectly fine.

Even in being familiar with a lot of what I was hearing, few feelings exceed that first experience of being thrust into a world that glides off the collective momentum it carries. What Nigerian youth culture possesses right now that few American scenes do is a vested interest in propelling their scene into global prominence. They're hungry to make a mark. I looked through the crowd. The young people here were all dressed similarly—vibrant soccer jerseys, baggy jeans, futuristic-looking sunglasses, beautifully patterned cornrows, and an abundance of crop tops—but even more noticeable was their collective exuberance. This was a crowd that was dancing, embracing one another, smiling at the acts onstage. No one was standing around too cool to rejoice. The cool thing to do here *is* to rejoice, to take part in launching this thing to the moon and be forever etched in history.

If my brains end up splattered across a Nigerian highway because my anxiety causes me to flee from these officers, or I become some sort of wannabe political prisoner here because they can't get a dime out of me, at least I would have been able to revel in an oasis of sanctified energy in my ancestral home region for a few hours, I think. But, as luck would have it, after three hours, Amarachi's contact made good on their promise to come rescue us from police custody. Still held in the back of our driver's truck, from the window I watch as a distinguished middle-aged gentleman with a button-down shirt, slacks, and an impressively moisturized bald head pulls up in a Mercedes SUV, walks over to the group of officers, who do all but genuflect to him, and exchanged a few words (and money, I assume). After they talk for about twenty minutes, an officer comes over and signals for me to roll my window down. "Sorry, sir, you have a blessed night and happy holidays," he says, handing me my passport and phone. I let out a sigh of relief after he walked away. A minute or two later he comes back and signals for me to roll the window down one more time. "This is yours, sir." It's my weed and a half-smoked joint he found under my seat. I laugh to myself and shake my head. They could at least have kept it to try to hide their extortionary intentions.

The next day, in need of less excitement, Ivie and I visit a place called the Jazzhole, a famed record shop and bookstore in a neighborhood called Ikoyi. The front of the shop houses all the music, such as a beautiful first-edition vinyl copy of the Lijadu Sisters' 1976 album *Danger*. I browsed through shelves, picking up whatever sticks out visually, since most of what I see is completely new to me. The place is owned by a husband-and-wife duo, the husband manning the music section while the wife sits behind the book section's counter. While I skim through the collection, I overheard the husband making small talk with Ivie, trying to guess where in Nigeria her family's from once he learns her name. "Where's his family from?" I hear him ask her, gesturing toward me.

"He's Black American," Ivie replies.

"Oh, really? I thought he was Nigerian."

I walk over and tell him that I'm unaware of my exact origins and am not fully comfortable with the concept of ancestry tests, especially since most don't have the capability of giving

you anything further than a country of origin, without speci-
fying the countless number of ethnic groups you might come
from.

"Well, we all know that it's somewhere in West Africa," he says.
"My advice is to travel to as many places in this region as you can,
and wherever feels the most like home is probably where you're
from."

Back in the bookstore section, I sit down to have a cup of tea
and flip through a book that sticks out called *Jailed for Life* by
Kunle Ajibade, a 1991 memoir from a Nigerian journalist who was
imprisoned for criticizing the country's tyrannical government.
As I read, waves of older women file in to catch up with the wife.
From behind my book, I observe their behavior: gossiping about
whose children have gone off the beaten path; letting out loud
*ooohh*ss when provided with scandalous information; professing their overbearing parenting styles; the particular way they're
hunched over the tables to relieve weight from their backs. Even
though I'm halfway across the world, I'm certain that I'm in the
presence of my grandmother and her sisters, or any Black aunties
I've witnessed throughout my life. I didn't feel this exact paral-
lel when I visited South Africa the previous two Decembers. But
here, in this little café on a calm Friday afternoon, I don't need
a resounding "Welcome home!" to feel like I've finally gotten the
opportunity to get close to the source of my being. The realization doesn't inspire tears more than it inspires a sense of calm,
a confirmation that I no longer need to try to fill a void. Sprin-
kled through this place are people whose faces and voices mirror
those of folks I see regularly back home. It is then that I realize
my Africanness isn't dependent on other people's distinctions; it

is just a fact of reality, even if my brach's recent station has been in America.

SEPTEMBER 2023

It isn't December this time and I'm not in Africa, but it is a beautiful Friday night in September, and I am at a packed Barclays Center in Brooklyn. I've planned on being here for months and could not imagine missing bearing witness to the magnetism of fast-rising star Asake, who, interestingly enough, has come into prominence by joining the best of sounds from his home country of Nigeria with amapiano, South Africa's newest evolution of club music—coincidentally the only two places on the Motherland I've visited. In 2022, he dropped his debut album, *Mr. Money with the Vibe*, and it marked a special shift in Black music. It's thirty minutes of the most invigorating music you'll ever hear at one time: danceable, steeped in spirituality, and, by definition, Pan-African.

Since I've been actively listening to youth-driven music out of West and Southern Africa for the past decade, I've always dreamed of what a global star with the ability to speak to all corners of the diaspora could look like. And we've had plenty of people flirt with the distinction. I'll disqualify Black Americans due to our culture being our country's most valuable export, subsequently forcing us onto others whether they like it or not. Dancehall star Popcaan seemed to have a real shot in the mid-to-late 2010s. Outside of the Black culture of the United States, Jamaica's Black culture has the most real estate across the globe, and Popcaan's charisma, hitmaking ability, and effortless coolness made him a strong contender. But his inability to tour the United States put a real damper on his global reach. One could say Nigerian star Burna Boy occupied that space for a few years. He aligned his career with the legacy of Fela Kuti, drew heavily from dancehall, had the fashion sense of an American rapper, and spent a portion of his upbringing in the UK. But no one has come close to the speed at which Asake has arrived in the running. Within a year's time, he's positioned himself for a historic run from within West African music's global expansion. Unlike Burna Boy, he barely bothers trying to speak English that is digestible to the masses, electing to mostly speak in his native Yoruba or in Nigerian pidgin. But the music is so electric, it doesn't matter.

At Barclays, the twenty-eight-year-old enters the stage in a sort of wired nest, the red glow of his motorcycle helmet glaring out through the cracks while dancers dressed in white march by his side and concertgoers cheer in anticipation. To start, he performs fan favorite "Organise," a song with a booming saxophone, tom drums, and what feels like a choir backing him. It combines jazz, gospel, fuji, and amapiano—modes of Black musical expression from various parts of the globe. I stand in the crowd in awe, in disbelief that someone so new to the scene could have this kind of reaction. What makes Asake's music especially impactful for me is his refusal to assimilate for the potential of crossing over. And why should he? If Bad Bunny can become one of the world's biggest artists by purely speaking Spanish, then a Yoruba-speaking artist with undeniably effective rhythms should be capable of the same.

The standouts from his two albums (*Mr. Money with the Vibe* and *Work of Art*) reverberat through the space. At every turn or transition into a new song, he looks out into the crowd, short in stature, but massive in star power, with smoke from a blunt coming out from his diamond-teeth-filled mouth. His dazzling outfit changes, dance breakdowns, saxophone solos from his supporting band, and an unexpected—but appreciated—moment with an infant nestled on his shoulder each lent themselves to the fact that he studied theater arts in college. And the experience of seeing him comfortable with juggling all that at once further confirms Asake as the diaspora's superstar.

For those of us who were made aware of Asake's artistry in 2022, his rise does feel rather meteoric, but he'd been devising a plan for a half decade by that point. He went from studying at Obafemi Awolowo University to trying to find his way within Lagos's underground creative ecosystem during the mid-2010s. During that era, he collaborated with Blaqbonez, who'd also go on to become a force in the Nigerian rap scene. The acoustic "Grind," from 2019, is revelatory, as Asake sings about how hard it is to find his way, even though he feels so close to fame. An ironic foreshadowing. His break came in early 2022 when street-pop-superstar-turned-label-exec Olamide hopped on "Omo Ope," which marked a shift in Asake's sound to bring elements of South African amapiano into the fold, joined with the foundations of street pop, Yoruba fuji music, gospel, and hip-hop. That formula—and Olamide's cosign and his label YBNL's venture with American label Empire—pushed Asake's music into a new stratosphere.

Whether it be "Peace Be unto You," "Sungba," or "Remember," his work creates a perfect storm of spiritual uplift and uncontrollable body movement, peppered with a hip-hop strut, in large part, to the rhythms coming out of South Africa's clubs. It's inspirational music for a new day; something that affirms Nigerian youth on the ground and draws in the country's large global diaspora as well as others within the wider global African diaspora that have an innate desire to connect with what's happening in the Motherland.

When he performs his hit "Joha," I look around to a crowd filled with first-generation West Africans and put forth my best attempt at singing in Yoruba. I get to imagine what it would feel like if I were fortunate enough to grow up speaking one of the mother tongues. But that I get to even try it inside an arena in New York City while jumping, laughing, smoking spliffs, and holding out gun fingers gives me a profound sensation of oneness; a sign that, after centuries separated, the diaspora is now able to mend what we haven't been able to construct on our own terms.

I thought back to the times I'd touched both Nigeria and South Africa, and how, now being at this Brooklyn show, the concept of home is changing into something different. If an artist like Asake can directly tie his ascendance to a very intentional mashing up of Nigerian, South African, and Black American forms of expression, then I think it's safe to say we've finally sailed to the future.

TIME IS VERY PRECIOUS

FROM CHILDHOOD TO MY early adult years, it was a near-daily practice for my family on my mother's side to convene at my grandmother's house after getting out of school or work. Even if just for an hour or so, it's how we kept track of one another as a unit. You never knew exactly what to expect. My grandmother, especially after her retirement, may have baked a couple almond pound cakes for us to take home. My daughter and niece might have had playdates with the other kids in the neighborhood planned for a few days. Or everyone might have a part to play in cooking a collective dinner. Roles changed as ages did. As I matured, I was becoming understood as the person in the family whose views were veering off the paved road: Christianity was no longer a belief system I subscribed to; out of respect for my queer friends, I called attention to second-nature homophobic remarks; and I was no longer hesitant to carry an aroma of weed coming into the house. The potential for argument or debate around any of the three was possible, but every now and then, I'd present something that everyone could agree on. I was aiming for my role to be someone who led the family in uncomfortable, yet transformative conversations by presenting them with the latest happenings in the digital world.

The late 2000s and early 2010s saw a rise in DIY, independently produced documentaries that were going straight to YouTube and lesser-known video-streaming sites. The first that took the internet by storm was a series called *Zeitgeist*, a weed head's dream of a documentary filled with theories around recent American wars, the "real" cause of 9/11, and the ways that Christianity was based on preexisting, astrology-influenced belief systems of the ancient world. But a series that was more insulated within the Black digital community, before it was easily infiltrated in the way it is now, was *Hidden Colors*. The premise of the series was to lift the veil off the ways Western forces had been working tirelessly for centuries to hide the ways Africans and their global diaspora contributed to human civilization. I'd already watched the first two with a couple friends at my apartment while we smoked jays and traded real-time commentary to what we saw. Coming from a family that enjoyed a good Paul Mooney stand-up or anything else that prioritized Black people's honor, I came to my grandmother's one day, summoned everyone to the basement, and connected my laptop to the television, where I showed them the series's first installment.

Hidden Colors doesn't have a coherent flow; maybe the desire for linear narratives is a Western construct, anyhow. From the gate, it stitches together clips of talking-head interviews with media personalities, independent scholars, and public speakers who are well-known in Afrocentric circles: Dr. Umar Johnson (years before he became a professional meme bank), Shahrazad Ali, Dr. Phil Valentine, Dr. Frances Luella Welsing. Each gets straight to the point, displaying specific ways they examine world history as it pertains to African contributions. With dramatic classical music playing in the background for impact, they touch on some well-known concepts. They speak about Mali's fourteenth-century ruler Mansa Musa, known for his considerable wealth and the legend that, on a trip through the Sahara, he gifted so much gold to Egypt that he threw the nation's economy off. They speak of eighteenth-century, Maryland-born Benjamin Banneker's supposed lineage to the Dogon people of Musa's native Mali as an explanation for his supposed penchant for astrology. And they speak about the pre-Columbian trips Africans made to the Americas.

Already having seen the film, I focused on my family's reactions. An assortment of "Mm-hmm," "Yup," and "Ain't that some shit" left their mouths with every tidbit of information offered. There was a sense of service I felt from being able to gather them for a greater cause—a restoration of Black pride that only really came out when day-to-day race relations were discussed. But with *Hidden Colors*, we got to collectively trade reflections about something most Black people in America feel: that, while living as subjects in a white-dominated society, we are, by nature of how this place runs, taken advantage of with regularity. Just a couple generations ago, my grandmother's father would likely have been a victim of predatory practices happening in Baltimore's steel mills, where white employees would be rewarded for Black workers' labor. Even in present-day news, we're learning about towns established for Black Americans that were systematically stolen by whites on a power trip, never to be heard about again (places like Bruce's Beach in California or Belmont in the DC suburbs). And when they are, the descendants of folks who risked their safety for better futures are given historical plaques in their honor. But rarely the land.

One of the documentary's talking heads called back to a sketch from *The Richard Pryor Show* in 1977. In it, Pryor is the only Black student on a team of archaeologists studying Egyptian pyramids. After he figures out how to open a tomb, the team (another member being a young Robin Williams) enters. A curious Pryor scans the inside with a magnifying glass and stops at an ancient book—*The Book of Life*. He hilariously decodes the pictographic story, instinctually: "In the beginning when man arrived on Earth, the Black gods that leave the spacecraft . . . and they named the beasts of the sea," he muttered before the truth became evident. "These were all Black people, God damn! Wait till the brothers hear this. I'ma get this book outta here, baby!" The white men in the group make eye contact with one another while Pryor experiences an awakening. They sneak out while he's reading and lock him inside to ensure the truth never gets out. It was such a perfect illustration to the feeling that being Black gives you here. That even craving the truth of ourselves can yield deadly consequences.

But, even as it's right on time in some instances, *Hidden Colors* takes a wild leap after its early moments of education. As soon as the documentary inches closer to the ten-minute mark (for reference, it's over ninety minutes long), the assertions being made border on comedy, especially in hindsight. Dr. Umar suggests that ninja culture originated in Africa and that the first samurai were, indeed, Black. "In Japan there's a saying that if you don't have a little bit of African blood, you can never truly be a samurai," he presents. Multiple interviewees point to rounded noses on ancient Buddha statues throughout South Asia as evidence of him being a man of African descent. Dr. Phil Valentine, with an air of certainty, says, in the ancient world, present-day Memphis, Tennessee, was part of the Egyptian dynasty, instead of the Memphis that was actually in Egypt. Though I can examine the film in hindsight with amusement, at the time I believed much of this had the potential to be at least somewhat true. If not fully. And so did my family as we watched. For a few years, as its popularity grew among people interested in history, the information offered in *Hidden Colors* provided talking points for serious conversations Black people shared around race.

In late 2012, I visited Baltimore's Walters Art Museum for a traveling show called *Revealing the African Presence in Renaissance Europe.* The exhibition's mission was to unearth previously hidden or skewed depictions of Black life in Europe between the fourteenth and sixteenth centuries. In one painting full of reds, blacks, and tans, the Alfama district of Lisbon, Portugal, shows Black people of various class distinctions: some in bondage, some noblemen riding horses in a courtyard. In another painting, one of the three Magi (from a Christian story connected to the birth of Jesus) is depicted as an African. So, too, are countless portraits of free Black people in French, German, and English works. As I walked through the Walters, scenes from *Hidden Colors* played through my mind. In this space, they were proven right: Black people's places in history *have* been erased. But as time went on, and more *Hidden Colors* films were released, the less I became able to withstand the ridiculousness of what they were selling. The more history books I picked up—about Africa and elsewhere— the more I realized the series as a harmful string of half-truths or straight-up lies. Its danger rested in that its thesis statement was true. Black people are forcibly kept out of the picture . . . but not in every society across the earth. In attempting to swell Black people with pride in our race and our contributions, the makers of *Hidden Colors* crossed a boundary that allowed them, in an attempt to build us up, to invalidate other nonwhite people by laying claim to their innovations. It's a hard pill to swallow that we've been fucked over, but the answer to that dilemma isn't to go around and do it to other people. Time is far too precious to set others back while we try to propel ourselves forward.

Talked to my boy on the phone the other day for the first time in a while. Once we got finished making sure the families were straight and administered wellness checks on each other, he decided it was crucial for him to reveal a concealed truth that I might not be privy to: "You know we not from Africa, right?"

An interesting way to redirect a conversation, but I entertained him. "What you mean?"

"So, I've been doing my research, and if you dig deep enough, you'll find that the vessels they claimed to bring people over here on weren't capable of transporting that many humans with eighteenth-century technology."

I held the phone in silence, not sure where this could go next. See, my boy moved out to the West Coast a few years ago, and one thing I know about niggas who move to the West Coast is that, in those first few years of relocation, the palm trees, access to clean eating, abundance of hikeable trails, and good-quality magic mushrooms start making them feel like they're not regular niggas anymore. So, I tried navigating the conversation with an open heart. I asked, "So if you don't think we came from Africa, where did we come from? I mean, the history is documented pretty well."

He tells me that we're actually indigenous to the Americas and, through centuries of manipulation at the hands of powerful white men, have been made to think otherwise to separate us from our true identity. And if we knew ourselves, we'd be able to fight to get our land back and secure sovereignty from the US government. By this point, I felt that my brother was being led astray, but I didn't make an ordeal out of it; just told him I didn't agree and that a simple look in the mirror would tell us we're both African.

From then on, I'd see him on social media signaling toward his new revelation: posting old illustrations of indigenous folks with skin tones closer to what we perceive as Black, probably from the mind of a conquistador; using the feather and bow-and-arrow emojis to mark himself Native; sharing unsubstantiated accounts from European travelers in the early colonial period of dark-colored people with thick hair. The heart tends to manipulate you into seeing whatever you desire, if you want it bad enough. To my boy, these were steps in the right direction of self-discovery—maybe even a confirmation. But, to me, all it said was a bunch of white people who had probably never seen anyone darker than folks from the Mediterranean encountered some butterscotch-shaded folks and thought, *This is the darkest person I've ever seen.* Or, these hypothetical explorers were somewhere closer to the equator and did see darker-skinned people. But race isn't just predicated on color. My dear friend also started sharing photos of Black Americans dressed in Native American garments, such as feathered headdresses, as more evidence of his new inclination. Black people throughout different periods of American history have been allied with and even adopted into Native culture, so being dressed in their drip isn't unprecedented. It also doesn't mean we can use those images to prove indigeneity. From what I could see, an obsession was starting to develop on his end, and I wanted to get to the root cause.

In 1976, the Guyanese scholar of Africana Studies, Ivan Van Sertima, released a book titled *They Came Before Columbus*, in which he spends the bulk of its pages proposing that Africans had traveled to the Americas on numerous occasions before the advent of the "New World." And, even further, he suggests the Nubian rulers of Egypt's twenty-fifth dynasty planned an expedition to the coastal civilizations of North Africa before a powerful current carried them westward, transporting them to parts of the Caribbean before reaching Mexico. In Mexico, these members of Nubia's elite encountered the Olmec tribe, who were, of course, not as advanced as they were. So, the Nubians gave them the keys to life—indirectly inspiring every Mexican civilization that followed the Olmecs—and went about their business. According to Van Sertima, the famous, colossal Olmec head sculptures originally found in Veracruz and Tabasco were made to honor the Africans who came to visit. The specimens' wide noses and big lips, in addition to pyramids and evidence of mummification in Olmec society, proved Black people from along the Nile's significance to pre-Columbian civilizations in North America. None of this has ever been confirmed at archaeological sites or supported by Van Sertima's contemporaries, but his book's popularity grew in the coming decades, especially with a rise in Black extremism that emerged to combat centuries of racial subjugation. Van Sertima's mission to confirm we were capable of technological advancement, innovation, and international influence before contact with European settlers was a righteous assertion, because it's true. But his method of execution teetered on the line of hyperbole and erasure, a tactic he learned from our enslavers without even noticing.

His book was divisive from the outset, hardly embraced by other scholars. In fact, it was often the subject of ridicule. In a 1977 *New York Times* review of *They Came Before Columbus*, the Welsh archaeologist Glyn Daniel accused Van Sertima of writing "with an abysmal ignorance of the prehistory of Europe and Africa." Twenty years later in the journal *Current Anthropology*, a group of scholars (Gabriel Haslip-Viera, Bernard Ortiz de Montellano, and Warren Barbour) published a paper titled "Robbing Native American Cultures: Van Sertima's Afrocentricity and the Olmecs." In it, they charged Van Sertima with pushing pseudoscience that served no one, but only his need to feel part of a superior group. By the nineties, his book was used as a source of pride in the curricula of majority-Black public schools and was being taught in Africana Studies programs at universities. Acknowledgment of the Olmec statues was making its way into Black-focused museums. As pointed out in the paper, challenges to Van Sertima's work mainly fell on deaf ears in the Black community because of a preexisting distrust of institutions of higher learning and the sciences. After all, these were the same institutions that, barely a century earlier, argued that people of African descent were an inferior subspecies of the human (white) race. But Haslip-Viera,

Ortiz de Montellano, and Barbour's most crucial criticism of the book's function was that, in attempting to depict Black people in a favorable manner, it effectively "diminished the real accomplishments of Native American cultures."

The deeper I saw my boy get into this line of thinking, the more my Instagram and YouTube algorithms started showing me people aligned with his newfound beliefs. He wasn't on a solo mission, screaming up at an empty sky; this was a digital-first community he'd been in long before he decided to fill me in on what was happening. From what I started observing, these folks, when talking about their indigeneity on social forums, lean on popular Black American tropes of having Cherokee grandmothers or distant Blackfoot relatives. Some organize in-person meetups where they visit national parks that display information about the various indigenous cultures that populated their grounds before being wiped out. Others, through a cryptic registration system, secure tribal ID cards that represent a group called the Yamasee and read TAX EXEMPT across the top. The Yamasee were an actual tribe of Native people from the present-day Southeastern states who waged war with settlers and rival indigenous groups before having to flee to Spanish Florida, where they formed communities with factions of Creek natives, Africans who'd escaped slavery, and Africans who were enslaved by the Creek. This band of groups became known as the Seminole Indians. This real history is obscured in present times to support people in my homeboy's orbit who subscribe to this new Native movement. Who's to say how people should identify? There's nothing wrong with honoring all parts of your heritage if you feel inclined to do so. But a problem I eventually discovered placed my boy and his Black Native community in the same territory as *They Came Before Columbus*, wiping another people's history out to engineer their own.

The most visible figure in this Black Native movement is Dane Calloway. He has over half a million YouTube subscribers and nearly five hundred videos, each made up of hours-long conspiracy theories that are more likely to give you a headache than draw you closer to your essence. In a slowed, performatively studious voice, accompanied by dramatic History Channel–like music in the background, Calloway seeks to cast doubt in his audience. Going through his channel, I click on one video where he's breaking down the movements of the Atlantic currents and how, based on those movements, it would have been close to impossible for enslavers to bring an abundance of people to the land we now occupy. In another, he alleges that the life of Harriet Tubman is a contrived story of bondage created during the 1860s to mislead Black people about their history. A reaction video from early 2024 features him focusing on the American Museum of Natural History closing two halls that displayed Native American objects, as they went against new federal regulations that require museums to secure consent from the tribes whose cultural artifacts they're displaying. Calloway thinks there's more to the story. To him, it isn't a coincidence that these exhibitions are coming down at the same time so many Black people are arriving to an understanding of their actual, indigenous lineage. And, the Native folks who are consulting on behalf of Eastern Woodlands and Great Plains tribes, according to Calloway, are foreigners co-opting the identity. And this is where the search for self turns into ideological colonialism.

I reached back out to my good brother, who's a fan of Calloway's rhetoric, once I emerged from the cloudy waters he luxuriates in. Cutting straight to the chase, I ask, "So, bro, if you believe the Black people here were already living on the land, then what about actual Native Americans? The ones we've understood as Native American our whole lives. Where do they fit in?"

He got National Geographic on me. "Those people have been here for a while as well, but they're a Siberian race who crossed a land bridge to get to this continent. We were *already* here."

Rolling my eyes, I sensed a passion in his voice when he emphasized the word *already*. It disappointed me. There's something to be said about experiencing life as leftover captives of war in a settler colony. About how, when your glasses are foggy, all you can see is the shame and embarrassment of descending from people who "allowed" themselves to be victimized in such a gutting manner. But if you apply some warm water and a cloth to those lenses, you'll be able to look at it from an angle that would underscore how much of a miracle it is that we get to bear witness (and experience) the depths of our determination to survive an all-out assault on our humanity. Because whom does it really serve for us to hijack the history of a people who, too, have suffered and continue to suffer greatly under the same oppressive regime? What do we look like trying their culture and contributions to society on like our latest costume in an attempt to distinguish ourselves from our very real past? Kinda sounds like a white person to me.

The deeper you go, the clearer the grift becomes. Dane Calloway is essentially running a digital cult, fully equipped with an operation that includes books, films, genealogy services, and songs that are all for sale. He is not a scholar, but he is savvy in the ways he disguises himself as someone advocating for truth.

The Yamasee ID my homeboy and a host of others paid for was the subject of a federal indictment in 2016 in which a Texas man, claiming to be the tribe's chief, was arrested for selling the cards to undocumented workers under the pretense of their using it to find work in the States. This isn't about getting in touch with your roots. It isn't even about Black people with actual indigenous ancestors who want to honor them properly. This is a textbook story of predator and prey. The prey being vulnerable humans wanting to feel whole, and the predator using those urges against them.

Time is very precious because, once again, I find myself traversing a corner of the internet that is being constructed to feast on Black people's insecurities. It's precious because the same people who run hood tourism YouTube pages, capitalize off our shame, and tell young Black men the only way to achieve any dignity is by denigrating Black women, the Black queer community, and Black immigrants are the same people radicalizing our Black men into pawns for the right-wingers' agenda to cause descent in groups they're most threatened by. And if we don't get our shit together with the quickness, we'll be acting on behalf of our own destruction while people like these grifters enjoy their spoils.

MIKE'S WORLD

THIS YEAR, AND EVERY year since the turn of the 2020 decade, has felt like an excruciatingly cruel series of events that, if you've been lucky enough to survive them, take chunks out of your flesh with every new tragedy. As I look back at 2024, which is three-quarters finished at the time of my writing this, it has been hard to celebrate anything when an active genocide plays out on our feeds at every waking hour, or your extremely over-qualified friends struggle to find consistent work, or another hip-hop icon dies of health complications before reaching old age. And this is on the heels of a pathogenic virus that spread across the globe killing millions while pushing others into varying levels of isolation and instability. We're all suffering, even those of us who refuse to say so. Perhaps the hope is that the constant onslaught of misery will somehow miraculously vanish. I suspect that won't be the case. And since it won't be the case, we are, more than at any other point my memory can produce, in desperate need of our community. Even when sulking feels like the easier option.

Only God knows the ways I've tried to hide myself from the people I love this year, only to revel in their company when pulled out of my slump. I think back to impromptu house visits on days

I couldn't shake the frustration of a check not coming through on time, where a few drinks and pop culture reactions extended relief to my clenched brow. Or to invites to hop on a train to Harlem for a dinner party where collaborative cooking provided sweet distraction from my misfortunes. Above all, one particular night emphasized, to me, the necessity of fellowship; how the power of collectively screaming out to a cracked sky when you've been corroding in your gloom can bring catharsis.

It was when upward of one thousand people happily crammed into New York City's Webster Hall back in May of 2024 to welcome their patron saint back home, the rapper who simply goes by MIKE. A perfect night was on the docket. He'd been touring through Europe and the United States for three months, and a week before the closing show at Webster, *You going to see MIKE Saturday?* texts started to file in from friends you only get to catch up with on occasion outside the digital world. It's like that every time he performs: making sure the people who dig him will be there, even though you already know they will, because nobody is just *kind of* into MIKE's music. To be into it is to love it, and to love it is to have an immense love for him because, for damn near a decade now, the brother has mastered the art of contextualizing what it feels like to experience grief and depression and uncertainty and, sometimes, a degree of introspection that fosters existential crises. And when he does express joy—which he's been doing a lot more of recently—it's a joy informed by the not-so-joyous times, rendering it triumphant.

My first encounter with his music was at a Fourth of July party back in 2018. He and his friends hosted it in a small empty lot in the Ridgewood section of Queens, and in between DJ sets and live cyphers on shoddy speakers, what became apparent was I'd stepped into a world that was already thriving, albeit new to me. Around one hundred kids, seemingly a decade my junior, decked out in niche streetwear brands, thrifted denim, and obscure jerseys, enjoyed one another's company and a modest selection of grilled foods. But when MIKE took hold of the mic, with his large frame and deep, monotone voice, chatter died down and all the attention shifted from the small conversation circles to his direction. He expressed gratitude for their continued support before shouting raps into the air—the smell of weed, grabba leaf, and the turkey dogs trailing through the space, too.

By this time, MIKE was already on a tear that suggested a fruitful career ahead. He had released three albums and a handful of shorter EPs to favorable reviews in the press, designating him the face of a new, youthful movement in New York City that expressed itself through poetically vulnerable lo-fi raps that were in conversation with art school jazz cats. On his first full length, 2017's *May God Bless Your Hustle*, songs like "armour" contained exultant soul-sample-looping production reminiscent of mid-2000s Kanye, while MIKE packed stories about being an impulsive, yet mentally sharp youth into succinct stanzas. "FOREVER FIND FLIGHT" from that same album is the type of track only someone staring at the possibilities of adulthood could make, as MIKE pledges to let his voice be heard, even in times of unsurety. His fear of being forgotten when his time is up rings through the track. You probably won't hear him rapping like this today since he's found a signature sound, but on songs like "Brick Blues" he approaches with a forceful assurance, suggesting that his physical body is starting to malfunction because he's left his soul on the page. Throughout, something greater is calling him to cry out to the world.

MIKE only got better with 2018's *Black Soap* and *Renaissance Man*, where he homed in on pairing vocals that hit like reflective phone conversations with production that is very much present. The chords often feel in support of the story, allowing his messages to land with a convincing poise. Those are the songs I heard at the cookout that day, and seeing their effect on the faces of his audience, I became a fan. There might have been moments when people's emotions led them to bounce around enthusiastically, but from what I can remember, everyone was impressively cool without performing a type of immovable stoicism; they were cool because MIKE was cool. And I love when the personality of someone's music is reflected in the people who care about it the most. They had the time of their lives, which was detectable in the big smiles on their faces as they watched the guy they came to see talk to them at eye level.

Over the years, MIKE has built a rock-solid catalog that, like the work of our best, has reflected the multidimensional truth of his life at the time of the music's release. After the loss of his mother in 2019, he released *tears of joy*, a record that felt like it came from someone weathering a storm. On so many of those songs—"TAKE CROWNS" or "Ain't no love" or "suffocate"—MIKE walks us through wet-eyed, weed-induced grieving while beats with severely chopped samples emphasize the pain. The self-produced *Disco!*, from 2021, still dealt with the weight of that loss, but showed him climbing out of a funk, energized by his ever-growing significance to the underground scene, which only became stronger as he continued to let listeners into his world.

On that album's opening track, "Evil Eye," he flicks away those who harbor ill feelings for him as he comes up for air after a trying period of life. The sample isn't necessarily up-tempo, but there's room for some shoulder movement, an improvement on how downtrodden he'd felt before.

In terms of career, it's been a steady climb uphill for MIKE since then. He's built out his 10k label to include like-minded artists from the States to the UK (Niontay from the Orlando area, Sideshow from the DC area, Jadasea from London). Under his producer name (dj blackpower), MIKE's released electronic side projects and made beats for Keiyaa and Liv.e, two of the scene's leading women, who make their own experimental takes on soul and R&B. He can list his idols Earl Sweatshirt and the Alchemist as friends and collaborators now. And MIKE's continued to release music that displays his dedication to his craft while establishing himself as a king in his world—someone who can be trusted to share the wealth because he's a genuine fan of what's happening. That trajectory—and the commitment to watering his fellow artists—is what led me and hundreds of others to Webster Hall that Saturday night.

The funk I'd been in felt a bit more manageable knowing this was where I'd end up for the night. I arrived with my homeys Timm and Andre, fellow MIKE enthusiasts with whom I got a late lunch within walking distance from the venue. When I'd seen MIKE back in 2018, it was thanks to an invitation from Timm, and now, six years later, we were still loyal members of the congregation. When we made it in, I kept running into other friends, each one confessing their hope for his setlists. Most wanted to hear the new shit, but as spaces filled with music nerds tend to get, others laid out the gems of his catalog they wanted to hear: loosies from *Renaissance Man*, a few from *Old Earth*, and, from me, as much *Disco!* as possible. I notice kids even younger than the ones I saw at that Fourth of July cookout in 2018; young ones firmly born in the twenty-first century, unironically wearing Fubu jerseys, backward visors, and frosted tips. Then I saw my friend Naz. We weren't expecting to run into each other, so when we did, we pulled each other in for a loving embrace. It felt kismet for me to hang out with her, a person who radiates in any space, throughout the show. I needed her cheerful energy around me, to both share our love for the music and to reminisce about times when I felt better. There was gratitude vibrating through the space.

When MIKE finally hit the stage in a crisp white tee and blue jeans, the crowd erupted. He expressed gratitude for being in this space; calling out that there was no better place to cap the tour than his home city. And then he ran through his very recent catalog: *Burning Desire*'s "98," "Mayors A Cop" with WIKI from their joint *Faith Is a Rock* tape, "World Market (Mo' Money)" from *Disco!* When MIKE performs, he doesn't have to exert much energy; he has a voice that's deep enough to extend through an entire building and a welcoming embrace, the type you can trust to lead you to a promised land within those boundaries. But when he landed on *Beware of the Monkey*'s "No Curse Lifted (rivers of love)," a personal favorite of mine—and presumably his—he instructed the crowd to up its energy. I looked over to Naz, and we both smiled, as if to sigh the words *Damn, this is a good night*. We yelled at MIKE's command and synchronized with the rest of the audience, reminded of our shared investment in a space held for a much-needed release.

It's in that moment when I found myself thankful for being alive in that particular time, in this particular mark in musical history—Black musical history—when artists who represent something counter to what the mainstream offers can thrive, but not in a self-righteous way. Shit, not even in a way that necessitates a uniform sound, or fashion sense, or place of origin. Only in the way that truly matters: which is trying to make every time someone engages with your work a transformative experience. I'm not sure that happens in the same way even if just thrown a few years into the past or future, but I know, in this concert hall, I feel temporarily alleviated from what's being weighing down on me.

I might not have given much thought to that reality if, earlier that week, I hadn't sat and repeatedly watched a minute-and-forty-three-second YouTube clip of the rap trio Digable Planets' acceptance speech at the 1994 Grammys, where they won Best Rap Performance by a Duo or Group. It must have come as a surprise that three New York City transplants from different parts of the country (Seattle, Philly, and the DC suburbs) could come together and be decorated with such an honor for the first single they ever released into the world, especially when stacked up against competition like Dr. Dre & Snoop's "Nuthin' but a 'G' Thang" and Naughty by Nature's "Hip Hop Hooray"—songs undoubtedly tied to the cultural specificity of their locales of origin that, at the time, felt like important rap anthems to anyone who encountered them.

While those two tracks, at face value, represented rap's bicoastal and untamable grit, Digable offered something more feathery with "Rebirth of Slick (Cool Like Dat)," a beautifully sleek number conceived from the confluence of hip-hop and its ancestor, jazz, that gave the mainstream world a glance into Brooklyn's bohemian scene, where college-educated negroes, curious souls in pursuit of enlightenment, and politically radical young adults uninterested in upholding the prevailing box office images of their communities occupied space. The song's video depicted a romantic, cinematic existence of the group's members (Ishmael "Butterfly" Butler, Mariana "Ladybug Mecca" Vieira, and Craig "Doodlebug" Irving), who gallivanted through the big city in black and white before descending on an intimate venue where they, backed by a fully equipped jazz band, perform the track. The lyrics, though fairly abstract, are in celebration of heritage and artistic skill—not dissimilar to the acts they were being pitted against at the Grammys.

But nonetheless, Digable Planets, from the time they released that single and the album it belonged to—1993's *Reachin' (A New Refutation of Time and Space)*—was being positioned as the antithesis of a rise in gangsterism, both in film and on records. Their approach to revolutionary sound was being framed as more progressive than that of the thugs coming out of the Five Boroughs, North Jersey, and Southern California because they didn't make magazine writers and record executives *as* uncomfortable as their kin. That'd probably explain why the good brother Butterfly, while notably working through some intense nerves, gave a speech that ended with "We'd like to accept this award on behalf of hip-hop music, Black culture in general . . . also we'd like to say to the universal Black family that one day we're gon' recognize our true enemy and we're gonna stop attacking each other. And maybe then we'll get some changes going on." He didn't want himself or his comrades to be perceived the way a *Time* writer did later that year when saying, "Rap is a form of rebellion, but it can be a trap when it plays into violent stereotypes. By adapting the humanism of jazz and channeling the power of rap away from antisocial braggadocio, Digable Planets are helping make hip-hop truly revolutionary." It was hard for the group to successfully shake that framing for the remainder of their brief existence.

Building off of what Butterfly said at the Grammys, later that year Digable released their sophomore album, *Blowout Comb.* It was a tangible, intentional shift in their approach. For one, in sound they distanced themselves from the progressive "jazz rap" label, meaning they weren't just sampling Black music that revisionist white critics appreciated since it was decades past its provocative heyday. And they weren't speaking in the same abstractions as they were that first go-round, either. *Blowout Comb* featured a more intense and affecting live instrumentation, adding an intensity that wasn't present in their previous work. Lyrically, the group responded to those critics' respectability accolades, articulating that, whether or not they hung out at cafés or rapped about shooting people, they were still susceptible to the same abuses of power the state exercised over them. "Black Ego" starts with what seems like a traffic stop where a cop calls Butterfly "boy" before everyone in the trio rhymes their take on the weight of being Black in this society; "Graffiti" frames them as part of a class of young people in NYC who skipped over college to express themselves through modes learned on the street; "NY 21 Theme" paid respects to the twenty-one Black Panthers (Tupac Shakur's mother, Afeni, being one of them) who, in 1969, were arrested in New York City and accused of planning to bomb and shoot two police officers. Digable Planets wanted there to be no confusion about where they stood, regardless of the *type* of rap they made.

In a review of the album in a 1994 issue of *The Village Voice*, dream hampton argued, "It's no great mystery that [Ladybug] Mecca and the Notorious B.I.G. both give shouts to Fulton Street. They live down the way from each other. It's the same hood and both Biggie and Digable place the community at the center of their universe." And it was true. Even though she could see that and Digable could see that, it didn't mean the world—or, more important, the merchants who package music in a way that promotes segregation and opposition—could see it, ultimately limiting the scope of what the Digable could be. *Blowout Comb* predictably didn't perform the way *Reachin' (A New Refutation of Time and Space)* did, not even receiving a *Billboard* certification after the debut went gold. It would be the second and final album the group released.

What I felt watching that Butterfly speech, thirty years later, was a sense of wonder, but also a fixation on what could have happened after that moment had the group been able to exist on their own terms, or even close to them; if they were able to operate how a MIKE can operate today. I was not even in preschool when Digable occupied the cultural space; my familiarity with, and appreciation of, their story is one of independent study. I do wonder, though, where I would have fallen in the conversation around their music and their role in the grand scheme of things had I been around. Would I have been in coffee shops that, by night, transformed into sanctuaries for spoken word? Would I have been forced, as a consumer, to choose an allegiance to one expression of Blackness as an attempt to signal what kind of negro I was? Would I identify with them at all? When I look around at today's hip-hop climate—at MIKE, Mavi, Navy Blue, Earl Sweatshirt, et cetera—I can't help but to identify where I see the spirit of Digable Planets among us. But unlike then, the guys occupying the counterculture space in rap today have the opportunity to steer the conversation in the way they want to have it.

In early 2024, MIKE dropped *Pinball* with New York producer Tony Seltzer, a stalwart in the underground rap scene whose chaotic, early-millennium computer-game-sounding production for DC's WiFiGawd is particularly exciting to me. On *Pinball*, MIKE pulls an audible on his audience. He is not the same reflective guy that people have come to know and love over the years. He is not in conversation with dreary loop-heavy production. Instead, he's shooting his shot at beautiful women, talking his shit, and delighting over the different strains of California weed he has access to. This came as a surprise to some critics and fans of his work, but for the most part, only to people who viewed him through a strict binary. Yeah, Seltzer crafted beats that he might make more readily available to the likes of Chicago's Lucki or Atlanta's Tony Shhnow, but MIKE has shown through his affiliations and people he chooses to champion or bring on tour that he's way more expansive in his thinking than just being some arbitrary mascot for so-called highbrow or intellectually stimulating rap music. He doesn't shy away from the type of music he likes to make, but never positions it as better than anything else. To me, it seems that MIKE peeps the chatter and is in active protest to whoever wants to place him in some sort of moral hierarchy. He also just wants to have fun. And as an independent artist engaging with the sound of the majority, he's doing what someone like dream hampton had to do on behalf of Digable thirty years ago. Back then, the group advocating to be absorbed correctly led to industry alienation and becoming fed up with the limitations of professional art-making.

At the end of the night after MIKE's Webster Hall show, I found myself just outside the venue in a huddle of intergenerational music journalists and enthusiasts, rejoicing in the beautiful experience we'd all just shared with a thousand other people. And then, behind me, I heard a familiar voice—albeit out of place— call my name. I turned around and it was my homeboy Josh, a photographer ten years younger than me from Baltimore, who said he caught a four-hour bus ride up I-95 by himself just so he could see MIKE close his tour, and to be in a space where people shared an excitement for what he contributed to the art form. It's what I wish every music show felt like. Rather than displaying the obnoxious urge to appear too cool or unmoved by what they see, real fans rejoice in that they can nerd out in person over some shit they'd spend endless hours on their laptops writing about. They sit on buses for hours by themselves to catch a show that means something to them. And they lean on their favorite artists to give them temporary alleviation from their troubles.

SALUTATIONS

L OVE TO RUNNING MAN, who, besides my own family, has been the only constant in my life. I wonder what it's like to have so much dedication, to say to yourself, "No matter what the weather is like, no matter how I'm feeling, no matter if all of my bills are paid, no matter if my feet don't even feel right in these shoes anymore, I am going to go out and jog around the whole Baltimore City until I am physically unable to take another step." I've seen the brother up Harford Road near the Wendy's, shuffling while I run into Walgreens for a bottle of water. I've seen him down on Green Street while I was taking a lunch break from my internship at SSA back in 2010. And I've seen him down the bottom of Park Heights in the rain. I've never seen Running Man walk, but one time I did see him standing. It was Artscape 2024 and the festival had been rained out. I was walking down Mount Royal before the light rail came down the street, bringing everyone to a halt. I scanned the crowd, as I tend to do, and there he was, looking unrecognizably normal. I looked at him, smiled, and said, "Aye, Running Man!" He didn't reply. But outside of that moment, even if it's just a shuffle, enough for his feet to leave the ground with every abbreviated stride, he doesn't take breaks. I think about what it takes to commit yourself to showing up in the world like that. Love to Running

Man, who in the past decade has been physically attacked twice. I don't know what would make a person want to hurt Running Man. The man don't even hardly slow down enough to fuck with anybody, and on two occasions someone has observed him, a symbol of discipline, a living urban myth, and decided to inflict physical violence on him. I get sad when I think about how often humankind takes its frustrations out on the most vulnerable— the ones they know won't fight back. No love to whoever had the cowardly inclination to do some shit like that.

Love to my sister, Amanda, my first hero. When she used to get punished, I would ask if she could still enjoy whatever pleasures I was about to enjoy, because I didn't like the idea of her being excluded. Love to my sister, Amanda, a tenderhearted woman whose tenderness has been used against her in ways that make me uncontrollably angry. One time when she was in high school headed back from a school trip, some of her classmates did some shit that teenagers do and threw eggs out of the bus window at cars on the road. An occupant of one of those cars called the police, and when the police instructed the bus to pull over, they came aboard and tried pressuring children into selling each other out. Once that didn't work, they became violent, punching little girls, attempting to break bones of young boys. From the back of the bus, Amanda saw a fellow student being violently pinned down by an officer, and when she ran to provide aid, a cop punched her in the face and attempted to break her arm while placing her in handcuffs. When the local news came to ask about what had happened, Amanda told the truth, but when the story aired, of course the truth never made the edit. It's interesting how they manufacture us for the public. Instead, charges were filed, and my sister was kicked out of all Baltimore City public schools. Fuck the police and fuck people who abuse children, knowing they won't face consequences. Love to my sister, Amanda, who, when we moved to Ramona, told me to stop watching so much TV, walked me outside to go talk to the other kids my age, and broke me out of my shell, changing the course of my life. Love to my sister, Amanda, who, whenever I needed a babysitter while trying to establish myself as a writer, going out to interview somebody or traveling for work, came through for me. Love to my sister, Amanda, for making me cringe every time she raps a song by some young new rapper whom I had no idea she was aware of.

Love to random road trips, their healing properties, and how much easier they make it to fall in love with someone. Two weeks after meeting my now wife, Armina, I sat over at my homeboy Greg's crib smoking a jay, drinking some random quarantine concoction we made up, listening to music when I mustered up some liquid courage. "Yo, I'm 'bout to ask this girl I been talking to if she wanna take a random ride with me." Greg gave me the nod of support. I asked her to ride to Assateague Island with me, speaking as if I were an expert on the place, though I'd never been. She agreed.

For those unfamiliar, Assateague Island is a majestic little place at the southern tip of Maryland's Eastern Shore—a little past Harriet Tubman's and Frederick Douglass's stomping grounds. To reach it, you have to cross the Bay Bridge, the most nerve-racking bridge in this country. But once you arrive, you'll be surprised to find this little patch of land that stretches between Maryland and Virginia is the home to some stunning wild horses—most of them sandy brown, with silky white or blond hair. Legend has it, some conquistadores from Spain wrecked a ship with these horses' ancestors aboard a few centuries ago, and over time the horses were never tamed and now they roam this little beach, fully protected. Love to the horses for escaping the grasp of colonizers. Lord knows, I wish my ancestors were successful at doing the same.

I made a strong case for myself on that trip, as it was the first time we spent stuck in one place together. I learned about her family, about what it was like growing up near the other side of the state, near DC. I learned how to be silent around her, which is extremely hard when you're getting to know someone. On the sand, we microdosed some shrooms and held each other's hands while lying in the sun, juice from a mango running down both our chins. When the sun was at its brightest, and we were at the height of our abbreviated trips, I looked over to her and got a good look at her side profile, outlined by the sun wrapping around her nose and brow. It's at that moment I fell in love and promised myself that I'd try bottling that feeling for as long as I could.

Love to Miss Tony, whose legendary status isn't measured by how famous they were or how many accolades they accumulated during their life. The most celebrated figures where I'm from are the ones who have been able to speak directly to the hearts of the people and their hometown roots. That rings true on a macro level, but it's especially apparent when looking at the legacy of music artists who have come out of the city. Some artists whose names barely ring a bell outside of Maryland's borders (or the Baltimore metropolitan area, for that matter) are heralded as deities here, while others who have gone on to make a name for themselves elsewhere are hardly mentioned by locals. Miss Tony, a pioneering figure in Baltimore's nightlife and club music scenes from the late 1980s to the mid-1990s, embodies that criterion.

Tony came up in the same hood that produced Freddie Gray and, according to family, danced and sang through their home and neighborhood. Sometime in the mid-1980s, when Tony was transitioning from adolescence to adulthood, they began to dress in drag and go by *Miss*—adorned in pump heels and beehive updos of the times. Love to the updo styles of the nineties and not the kind they showed in John Waters movies. I'm talking about the ones from our side and how iconic they still look in photographs, decades later. Tony naturally drew attention from their peers and didn't waste an ounce of it. They channeled that energy and expelled it in a developing underground nightlife scene where breakbeats from Chicago and New York house records were being isolated, sped up, and looped by local DJs and producers. Love to Chicago house, New York house, Miami bass, and drum & bass out of London. If not for them, we don't have Baltimore Club. Without them, Tony doesn't set history on its course by becoming the first person to regularly lay vocals over club beats. Love to Tony for trailblazing.

Love to *remembered rapture* by bell hooks, a book about writing that I couldn't put down while tryna make myself a better writer. Love to how, more than anyone else I've read so far, hooks has this uncanny ability to yoke you up like an aunt who sees you acting out in the back pews of the church and tells you to do better. Be better. My aunt Marie used to do that; she had a constant stutter and her go-to method of physical discipline was to smack you on the lips if you kept talking, but when she popped you, it was in the rhythm of her stutter. So, one slap to the lips was really about nine really fast slaps. Love to bell hooks for making me think about my aunt Marie. She passed on while me and my lady were on another pandemic road trip, this time to the sea islands of South Carolina, feeding ourselves with some good, historical (and futuristic) negro culture. Love to *remembered rapture* by bells hooks because, in it, she leaves us with this to chew on: "Writers from marginalized groups are usually faced with two options: overidentification with an identity or disidentification." I don't know about you, but the last thing I ever wanna do is to "disidentify" with my niggas. But then, I also don't wanna be one of those niggas overly laying on a Twitter-informed rendition of Blackness that then turns into a cheesy idea of how nuanced Blackness really is. But anyway, love to bell hooks for writing that book.

Love to the power of wandering around New York City with absolutely nowhere to go. There's a lot to complain about when it comes to that place—the whirlwind of smells that hit you soon as you step outside, the way people who just moved into entire Brooklyn brownstones don't ever speak because they figure avoidance is the better option, the way the NYPD kills its own citizens over not paying $2.90 to get on the train when it's almost fucking impossible to even afford a room to lay your head at night, the way I saw a mangy rat hobbling around the lobby of my building the day I was moving—but there's no other place on earth I'd rather aimlessly walk for hours. Love to the endless iterations of Blackness you encounter there daily and how, contrary to what they say about the place, those Black people are never cold toward you when you come correct. Unless, of course, they're having a bad day, which is easy to have in a place that demands the majority of its population to work itself to exhaustion just to make it to the next week. Or the next day.

Love to my favorite songs right now, which I'm gonna break down for y'all. Love to "Ozeba" by Rema, which, to me, sounds like the future and the sacred ancient past all at once. That boy is the future of Black music, not just Nigerian music or African music. Love to how, when niggas thought they had my boy figured out, he hit a full 180 on them. When he came out as a nineteen-year-old at the close of the last decade, there was a suggestion that he would follow in the footsteps of a Wizkid type—incredibly smooth, baby-faced, sweet vocals about love, sex, and general enjoyment. But on his new album, *Heis*, is dark, high energy, not easily tied to any particular trend, outside of a general movement toward making music more danceable. Love to his making a "don't think you have me figured out" kind of play.

Love to those Florida boys Luh Tyler and Loe Shimmy, who, on their song "Aretha Franklin," luckily don't shame our soul angel with disrespectful associations to her name. Unless you consider their making a play on words that changes the significance of her last name to mean they're stacking up $100 bills because Benjamin Franklin's face is printed on them. Love to them boys for mastering a fluidity of delivery that makes your body writhe with the words. And love to when Shimmy said he's gonna express his feelings and "jump on this bitch with some passion." That's how I'm coming with everything I write.

Love to Jorja Smith and Lila Iké for their angelic execution on "Greatest Gift," a measured and sincere attempt at reassuring to a lover that regardless of whatever place they find themselves emotionally, or however difficult (or pleasant) life gets, they'll be loved, appreciated, and looked after with the utmost care. I hope my love feels like that.

Love to the people of Gaza and the West Bank and the Congo and Haiti and Sudan. People whose public executions—being burned alive, their children shot at point-blank range, their only remaining hospitals burned, and their access to nutritional sustenance denied—have been put on Main Street for us all to see, though many will still pretend that they don't see what's in front of them. Instead, they try to find ways to both-sides the situation when, really, it's one side, which is the side of humanity and the side of decency and the side of not displacing people because you have a passionate bloodlust for domination. Love to never feeling like you're incapable of enduring a similar fate just because you live within the boundaries of empires that control the chessboard. And love to not being tricked into taking the side of the same oppressors who only tolerate you because there's a more recent group of people to brutalize in the name of expanding the empire. It's too late in the game to be that delusional. Love to people who endure the ugliness of greed that we're so often living at the fingertips of. Love to people who, when it looks like there is no hope, continue to fight against genocidal regimes. Love to people who have risked their livelihoods and lives to speak out against brutality against innocent women, men, children, legacies, and histories. Love to future generations that will continue the resistance, because the resistance doesn't die with individual life cycles. Love.

ACKNOWLEDGMENTS

INFINITE GRATITUDE:

To Armina and Ayden, my leading ladies and the ones who've had to hear about this book and its challenges, potential, and stakes for far too long. Not sure where I'd be without the round-the-clock familial support.

To my dearest friends Shan, DeeJ, Abdu, Devin, and D Watkins for always taking that phone call, extra read, and extra time to sooth me throughout this process. For pushing me in ways I was hesitant to push myself.

To my writing community: Andre G, Timmhotep, Shamira Ibrahim, Alphonse Pierre, Dylan Green, Ivie E. Ani, Marcus J. Moore, Akiba Solomon, Mankaprr Conteh, and Ben Dandridge-Lemco for the continued commitment to hold one another up through the ups and downs of this thing we chose to do with our lives.

To my agent, Will LoTurco, for reaching out to me in 2021 and putting the initial battery in my back to embark on this book-making journey.

To my mother, my father, and my uncle Derrick for everything.

NOTES

A VERY PRECIOUS TIME

1   *That's where they put you when they don't see you*": Paul J. Macarthur, "Catching Up with Gil," *Houston Press*, September 3, 1998, https://www.houstonpress.com/music/catching-up-with-gil-6569714.

MY KING, MY FATHER

43   *various stints in group homes*: Koopsta Knicca, "Koopsta Knicca on the History of Three 6 Mafia aka Triple 6 Mafia, Talks About His Beef with DJ Paul," Koopsta Knicca Video, YouTube, June 7, 2023, at 18:48, https://www.youtube.com/watch?v=xrEPLoZ8nRU&t=551s.

A LOVE LETTER TO STEAMED CRABS
PILED ONTO A BED OF NEWSPAPER

53   *the US citizenship of anyone holding it*: *Acts of the Fourth Congress of the United States*, Chap. 36, "An act for the relief and protection of American Seamen" (Philadelphia, 1796), https://tile.loc.gov/storage-services/service/ll/llsl/llsl-c4/llsl-c4.pdf.

53   *Black people's increasing liberation and influence*: *Maryland Session Laws*, Chap. 323 (Annapolis, 1832), https://msa.maryland.gov/megafile/msa/speccol/sc2900/sc2908/000001/000213/html/am213--445.html.

57   *other found objects*: Wiley A. Hall, "Eloquence, Humor Define Artist's Cultural Cre-
      ations," *Baltimore Sun*, February 16, 1995, https://www.baltimoresun.com/1995/02
      /16/eloquence-humor-define-artists-cultural-creations/.

58   *over ten years*: John Dorsey, "Tom Miller, Behind the Smiles," *Baltimore Sun*,
      February 27, 1995, https://www.baltimoresun.com/1995/02/27/tom-miller-behind
      -the-smiles/.

REVISITING RAMONA

89   *an old neighbor of mine, said to me*: t.p. Luce, *Tha Bloc: Words, Photographs and Bal-
      timore City in Black, White and Gray* (Baltimore: Obie Joe Media, 2004), 30.

MR. MOONEY & THE COMPLEXION
FOR THE PROTECTION

131   *separated from its violent origins*: Paul Mooney and KRS-ONE, "When the 'N' Word
      Is Part of a Routine," interview by Farai Chideya, *News & Notes*, NPR, November
      30, 2006, https://www.npr.org/2006/11/30/6560171/when-the-n-word-is-part-of-a
      -routine.

BRUISED

160   *equal parts shameful and arresting*: Miles Warren, "SVFF Q&A with Miles Warren
      (Director of *Bruiser*)," Sun Valley Film Festival, January 10, 2023, YouTube, at 19:47,
      https://www.youtube.com/watch?v=0sBnV5rXomo.

MIKE'S WORLD

221   *himself or his comrades to be perceived*: Christopher John Farley, "Music: Cats &
      Rappers," *Time*, November 21, 1994, https://time.com/archive/6726361/music-cats
      -and-rappers/.

222   *limiting the scope of what the Digable could be*: dream hampton, "Kiss Yourself Good-
      bye: A New Refutation of the Alternative Nigga," Village Voice, November 28, 1994.

ABOUT THE AUTHOR

LAWRENCE BURNEY is a writer, critic, and the founder of *True Laurels*, an independent magazine covering Baltimore's music and culture scene. His work has appeared in publications such as *New York* magazine, *GQ*, and *Pitchfork*. He has also worked at *The Fader*, VICE, and *The Baltimore Banner*. *No Sense in Wishing* is his first book. Follow him on Instagram and X @TrueLaurels.

Atria Books, an imprint of Simon & Schuster, fosters an open environment where ideas flourish, bestselling authors soar to new heights, and tomorrow's finest voices are discovered and nurtured. Since its launch in 2002, Atria has published hundreds of bestsellers and extraordinary books, which would not have been possible without the invaluable support and expertise of its team and publishing partners. Thank you to the Atria Books colleagues who collaborated on *No Sense in Wishing* as well as to the hundreds of professionals in the Simon & Schuster advertising, audio, communications, design, ebook, finance, human resources, legal, marketing, operations, production, sales, supply chain, subsidiary rights, and warehouse departments who help Atria bring great books to light.

Editorial
Kate Napolitano
Hannah Frankel

Jacket Design
James Iacobelli

Marketing
Zakiya Jamal
Morgan Pager
Aleaha Renee

Managing Editorial
Paige Lytle
Shelby Pumphrey
Lacee Burr
Sofia Echeverry

Production
Abel Berriz
Fausto Bozza
Steve Boldt
Yvonne Taylor

Publicity
Joanna Pinsker
Annie Probert

Publishing Office
Suzanne Donahue
Abby Velasco

Subsidiary Rights
Nicole Bond
Sara Bowne
Rebecca Justiniano